USES & ABUSES
of SOCIAL RESEARCH in SOCIAL WORK

Tony Tripodi

USES & ABUSES
OF SOCIAL
RESEARCH
IN SOCIAL WORK

Columbia University Press

New York and London   1974

COPYRIGHT © 1974 COLUMBIA UNIVERSITY PRESS

LIBRARY OF CONGRESS CATALOGING IN PUBLICATION DATA

Tripodi, Tony.
Uses and abuses of social research in social work.
Includes bibliographical references.
1. Social service-Research. 2. Social service.
3. Sociological research. I. Title
HVII.T75   361'.007'2   73–17280
ISBN 0-231-03662-0
ISBN 0-231-03663-9 (pbk.)
PRINTED IN THE UNITED STATES OF AMERICA

to
Joe Torchia

Foreword

~·~

This book is about knowledge, how it is generated through social research, and how it can usefully and appropriately be examined so as to inform social work practice. This is an especially important book for the student, educator, and practitioner of social work, for it provides an unusually clear understanding of the nature of research knowledge, thereby serving to enhance both education and social practice.

A key component in education for social work is the acquisition of knowledge that can be applied in professional practice. At present levels of development and utilization, research knowledge can only contribute in a partial way to the social practitioner's activities, but this contribution is recognized as exceedingly significant for present and future practice. For example, research knowledge from the social and behavioral sciences is now incorporated to a considerable degree in the professional curriculum of schools of social work. The increased infusion of behavioral science knowledge into social work literature is dramatically illustrated in edited books and selections appearing in social work journals of the past decade.

Yet, the lag between knowledge development and application remains a serious obstacle to effective social work practice. Professor Tripodi's *Uses and Abuses of Social Research in Social*

Work is directed toward diminishment of this lag, and he provides a much needed perspective for the development of research utilization skills by social workers. His work is of particular import in a time of an acceleration of knowledge production relevant to social work, and in a time of changing practice methods, demands, and societal conditions. The task of understanding, selecting, and assimilating knowledge from research for social practice under changing conditions is a difficult one. The task is facilitated now in large part by Tripodi's work. Here in a single volume the reader is presented with a basic description of the process of social research, criteria for evaluating knowledge from research, and a thorough consideration of factors related to the use and abuse of the results and methods of social research. This combination of materials results in a systematic framework which builds on a wealth of research literature, and which offers an invaluable guide to research utilization.

Tripodi's work is particularly salient for social work education, since the curriculum policy statement for master's degree programs in social work states that "A concern for the development of new knowledge and the testing of generally accepted principles, formulations, and hypotheses should be evident in the entire curriculum. The student should be encouraged to question constructively all aspects of the body of knowledge which is transmitted in education for social work practice (and the professional knowledge which is inherent in that practice)." This book will serve the student and educator well in their quest for and questioning of knowledge in the social work curriculum. The development of new knowledge relevant to social work practice presently rests, in the main, with educators and researchers, not with practitioners. Yet, the curriculum policy statement for schools of social work includes as a major goal of social work education the provision of a basis for students to "utilize scientific and scholarly inquiry in advancing professional knowledge and improving standards of practice." Tripodi speaks directly to this objective, and contributes to a growing literature on research of import to the social worker and the social work researcher. Particularly noteworthy in Tripodi's work is his incisive grasp of both social work practice and social research, and his exposition of their relationship. While this theme is evident throughout the book, it is highlighted in his final chapter on facilitating research utilization, which deals with the conduct of practice-related research, and the conduct of research utilization.

Combined with his earlier volumes on research, Tripodi's work becomes one of the landmarks in the University of Michigan's School of Social Work's pursuit of the objective of advancement of basic and professional knowledge attuned to social work education and social work services—an objective which includes goals for basic and applied research and for the scholarship that embodies the knowledge derived from organizing and conducting learning experiences with students. In this achievement, Tripodi reflects the special spirit of Michigan which emerges as the School seeks to integrate its goals of social work education, knowledge development, and public service.

Phillip A. Fellin, *Dean*
School of Social Work
The University of Michigan

Preface

~·~

The purpose of this book is to facilitate the process of research communication in social work by indicating how social research information might be effectively used, rather than abused. It is intended for undergraduate and graduate students in social work who are being introduced to social research and its possible uses. Moreover, it is hoped that the organization of ideas in relation to the uses and abuses of social research will be instructive for both social researchers and social workers.

Chapter 1 serves as an introduction to social research, and to the relationship of social work to social research. It includes a number of concepts and ideas basic to the subsequent chapters. In chapter 2 a framework is presented for practitioners and social researchers to use similar criteria in discussing and evaluating knowledge from social research. Chapter 3 is devoted to the articulation of important dimensions to be considered in the process of communicating and implementing social research findings; while chapter 4 is concerned with the use of social research techniques to meet information-gathering and-processing demands in social work practice. To further increase the effective use of social research, chapter 5 indicates the kinds of abuses that could occur in the transmission and receipt of research information. Finally, chapter 6 deals with the facilitation of research utilization by presenting five models for conducting practice-related research and by discussing five modalities for the conscious planning of research utilization by social workers.

The ideas presented in this book are derived from the literature and from my observations and experiences in teaching, conducting research, and providing consultation on research and evaluation to a variety of social agencies. In addition, my thinking has been influenced by the following persons: Phillip Fellin, Henry J. Meyer, Edwin J. Thomas, Irwin Epstein, Roger Lind, John Ford, Richard B. Stuart, Jack Rothman, Frank Maple, Charles Garvin, and Paul Glasser—all of the University of Michigan; Alfred Kadushin and Sheldon D. Rose of the University of Wisconsin; David Fanshel, Alfred J. Kahn, and Samuel Finestone of Columbia University; Henry Maas of the University of British Columbia; Scott Briar of the University of Washington; and Ernest Greenwood of the University of California, Berkeley.

I am grateful to Dean Phillip Fellin and the University of Michigan for granting me a sabbatical leave for the purpose of completing this manuscript. In particular, I wish to acknowledge the editorial assistance of my wife, Mrs. Roni Tripodi, and of John Moore and Joan McQuary of Columbia University Press; and my thanks to Mrs. Joyce Morgan for typing all portions of the manuscript, and to Miss Kathleen Waite for assisting in the preparation of the index.

Tony Tripodi

August, 1973

Contents

USES & ABUSES
of SOCIAL RESEARCH in SOCIAL WORK

Chapter 1

~·~

Social Research
and Social Work

Social work is a helping profession which uses a variety of information from its own discipline, other helping professions such as education and psychiatry, and the social sciences. Its aims are to improve the social functioning of individuals and groups in organizations and communities, and to formulate and implement social policies designed to increase the responsiveness of social agencies and communities to the needs of client groups.[1] The tasks of social workers can be differentiated by referring to the traditional demarcation of social work methods as social casework, social group work, community organization, and administration and policy development.* Although there are cur-

---

* Social work education and social work research are not included in this classification for two reasons: 1) as reflected in the catalogues of schools of social work, they are not typically regarded as methods of social work practice; 2) the proportion of social workers engaged in such activities is relatively low.

rent movements to develop new roles for social workers and to combine methods (e.g., social casework and social group work into social treatment), most available jobs for social workers are advertised and classifiable by the traditional designation of social work methods above. Furthermore, authors of recent social work texts employ this classification in their presentations.[2]

Functions and Activities
of Social Workers

Social caseworkers work primarily with individuals and families in a variety of social settings—family agencies, correctional institutions, parole and probation departments, public welfare, medical and psychiatric clinics and hospitals, drug abuse programs, and so forth. They provide assistance by helping clients make decisions to improve their life circumstances, by advocating for institutional and community changes in relation to their clients' needs, and by referring clients to appropriate resources such as medical, financial, and legal aid. The primary vehicle of social casework practice is face-to-face interviewing with clients, their families, and other significant persons in their lives. Often the objectives of social casework are attitudinal and behavioral change, and various therapeutic techniques such as behavioral therapy, problem-solving modalities, and crisis intervention may be employed.[3] Social caseworkers assess the circumstances of their clients' psychological and social situations, formulate with their clients the objectives of casework treatment, develop plans for accomplishing such objectives, and implement those plans.[4]

Social group workers have objectives similar to those of social casework in that they attempt to achieve goals of individual growth and change among their clients. The primary context is, however, through discussion in a group. The number of clients in a group depends on the purpose and function of the group as determined by the group worker and the group members. Some groups are structured for purposes of educational and recreational activities, where the group size may be larger than fifteen members, while other groups are set up for the purpose of attitudinal and / or behavioral change and may have as few as three group members. Group workers employ techniques derived from group dynamics, small group psychology, learning, and personality theories. Thus, they may use role playing, group consensus, techniques for monitoring the progress of individuals, and so forth.[5] Group workers also use face-to-face interviewing with individual members of the group, typically to learn about the strengths and weaknesses of those members and their goals in relation to the group. The group worker determines the appropriate size and composition of the group necessary to achieve the goals of individual members and of the group, and he plans the group meetings to maximize the contributions of each of the group members.

According to Rothman, community organization is classifiable into three modes of practice: locality development, social planning, and social action.[6] Locality development has as its goal community change by means of a wide participation of people at the local community level. It aims to create conditions of economic and social progress through such activities as neighborhood programs fostered by settlement houses. Social planning is devoted to the gathering of facts about social problems, such as blighted housing conditions, and to the articulation of a rational plan for alleviating those problems. While locality development and social planning are based primarily on a strategy of consensus among interested community groups, social action is based on conflict and confrontation. It seeks to provide more power to disadvantaged groups in the population by means of their organization and through their demands for increased community resources. The aim of social action is to achieve basic community and institutional change.

Community organizers initiate meetings with community representatives, social agency administrators, disadvantaged persons in slum neighborhoods, etc. They attempt to foster the process of community self-determination by locating key persons and groups and by helping them to organize around relatively important community issues, such as the bureaucratic red tape involved in the administration of welfare programs. In their work with communities, community organizers amass facts related to community needs and resources, locate inequities in public ordinances, and collect other basic information on community issues and problems. They may use strategies of locality development, social planning, or social action in attempting to solve community problems.

Policy developers locate and plan broad policy changes that affect the distribution and delivery of social work services. They work with the loci of power, legislators and other political figures, as well as through professional and governmental organizations. Policy developers are usually involved in social planning and administrative activities. Administrators are responsible for operating and planning the services of public agencies and for monitoring the operations of their agency personnel. A good deal of an administrator's time is spent in planning for annual budgets and locating possible resources for funding. In addition, administrators develop and implement personnel policies and practices, arrange for the efficient allocation of resources, and prepare written and oral presentations to persons or groups which have fiduciary responsibility for the agencies they head.

Social Work Accountability

Social work as a profession is accountable for the work it does with and for its various constituencies. The social caseworker and group worker are responsible for their interventions with individuals and group members, and they are accountable for their actions and decisions. The clients have a right to know the extent to which the techniques employed in casework or group work are successful, innocuous, or potentially harmful. Participants in community organization are concerned about whether their time and energy are usefully spent in relation to the achievement of social and institutional change. Legislators, public officials, and community representatives are interested in the effectiveness and efficiency of new and existing activities of social agencies; and administrators, social planners, and policy developers are accountable to such persons. Thus, social workers are accountable to their clients, community representatives, funding bodies, their fellow professionals, and the general public.

Social work accountability implies that the profession of social work is responsible for indicating the extent to which its services are necessary and desirable for individuals, groups, and organizations. Accountability means that "practice must be open to the scrutiny of colleagues in order to get new perspectives and in order for 'error' to be corrected and brought to light." [7] A profession such as social work can only be accountable if it pays close attention to examining its activities in relation to effectiveness and efficiency in achieving client goals. Moreover, a profession is accountable to its constituencies if it provides public information related to the discarding of ineffective procedures and to the development of more viable methods for achieving its goals.

As indicated by Loeb, accountability can be accomplished by information secured through evaluation techniques, and more specifically through social research.[8] Evaluation is geared to providing information about the efforts, effectiveness, and efficiency of social work programs and activities; and experiments, surveys, and case studies are social research strategies that can be employed for such purposes.[9] In addition, social research can be employed as a tool to answer questions related to the functions of social work practitioners. An illustrative sampling of these questions is as follows:

1. Are black social caseworkers more or less successful than white social caseworkers in promoting behavioral changes in black communities? white communities?
2. To what extent is the behavior of individual members in group work sessions related to their behavior at home?
3. What is the optimal duration of casework or group work intervention for changing the behaviors of children who have adjustment difficulties in school?
4. What is the relative efficacy of social casework as opposed to group work for the rehabilitation of delinquent youth?
5. To what extent is a social agency's services applicable to the needs of its potential clientele in a specific community?
6. To what extent are public assistance recipients likely to

work as a function of different types and amounts of wage incentives?

7. To what extent and under what conditions are pressure group tactics likely to lead to social change?

8. Is it more efficient to employ part-time or full-time workers?

9. To what extent are attempts to coordinate a multiplicity of services more or less efficient than services not coordinated?

10. What conditions facilitate or impede the introduction of a new technology within a developing locality?

11. What are the medical, legal, social, and financial needs of the residents of a particular neighborhood?

12. What is the relative effectiveness of black, white, and chicano community organizers in organizing white lower middle-class groups?

13. Are process recordings, summary recordings, or behavioral check lists efficient and effective in providing information necessary for the achievement of casework or group work goals?

The Relationship of Social Work to Social Research

THE CONDUCT OF SOCIAL RESEARCH BY SOCIAL WORKERS

Although social workers ascribe to the notion of accountability and although there are a number of research questions pertinent to social work practice, there has been little investment in the conduct of social research by social workers. Indeed, Morris has stated that "Social work functions with the lowest investment in research and development of any major enterprise in the United States — perhaps less than .003 percent of the sums being planned for." [10] The vast majority of social workers have not been trained to initiate and carry out research, and social work personnel engaged in research are primarily those few persons with doctoral degrees who have received advanced training in social research.

Probably, less than 1 percent of social work manpower is actively engaged in research, which is a basic reason for the relatively small volume of research that has been reported in the social work literature. However, content analyses of social work periodicals in the 1950s and 1960s have revealed that an increasing percentage of the articles reported are devoted to research and evaluation.[11] Illustrative of this trend, it is notable that the volume of the journal *Social Work* for 1970 contained 48 articles of which 37.5 percent were reports of research and of which an additional 37.5 percent included references to research findings.

Many social research studies pertinent to social work have been conducted by professionals other than social workers— sociologists, psychologists, public health researchers, management analysts, and so forth. Indeed, much of the research related to social work has been conducted by social scientists with social work interests, rather than by practicing social workers. This has led to discussions about social research and social work practice as separate enterprises and about conflicts between researchers and practitioners.[12] Conflicts have arisen from two basic sources: perceived differences in objectives and the perceived threat of evaluation. Practitioners are typically concerned with immediate decisions of their practice, while researchers proceed cautiously and methodically in their work. Moreover, research is perceived as threatening if it has the function of evaluating practice, for it might lead to decisions that would affect the conduct and nature of that practice. Thus, a dichotomy has been set up between research and practice. However, this conception has not been useful for social work and, as pointed out by Briar and Miller, it is false.[13] First of all, most social work intervention can be characterized as incorporating components of scientific method analogous to those employed in social research. Second, evaluation of social work activity is a professional responsibility subsumed under the notion of accountability. Third, social research is a tool which can aid practitioners to examine their practice and to determine what kinds of information are useful for practice decisions.

The extent to which social research is or is not relevant to social work practice depends upon the phenomenon being investigated. Social research contains a body of techniques and procedures for generating knowledge; and if the object of research is to study aspects of social work practice, it is obviously pertinent. In fact, there are many social work scholars who argue that research is simply a component of practice. Zimbalist indicates how the community practitioner is involved in fact-finding and community assessment by utilizing survey techniques and other methods.[14] Fanshel points out that the development of knowledge related to social needs and resources is essentially part of the social planning and administrative process.[15] Schwartz argues that group work practitioners should systematically compile and evaluate information pertaining to their practice, while Rose utilizes monitoring techniques based on research principles for assessing clients and their outcomes in the behavioral group treatment of parents and children.[16] And, finally, new developments in social casework, such as behavioral modification, require that data be systematically collected and analyzed by techniques used and derived from social research.[17] Although it is probable that only a small proportion of social work practitioners actively incorporate research methods in their practice, research studies directly related to intervention techniques are increasing.

In a recent volume devoted to reviews of research in social work during the latter half of the 1960s, Rothman indicates that there are beginning efforts for producing research directly related to strategies of community organization and social planning, and he develops a number of research hypotheses in that regard.[18] In addition, both Schwartz and Briar indicate that there are more studies directly related to evaluation and the techniques of practice than in previous years.[19]

It is especially interesting to compare reviews of research in family casework by Briar in 1966 and in 1971.[20] He pointed out in 1966 that much of social casework actively involved participation in the process of supervision, but there was little research in that area. Hence, he called for more research in supervision. Briar's subsequent review of research in 1971 indicated there

was still little research in supervision despite his previous recommendations. Evidently, the research review was not utilized.
Furthermore, it is quite possible that most family service caseworkers did not read his review in the first place!

THE UTILIZATION OF SOCIAL RESEARCH
BY SOCIAL WORKERS

In his exhaustive review of studies pertaining to the use of
research information from the social sciences, Brittain concluded
that "The question of the application and utilization of research
data is of paramount importance to all the social services, and
certainly to social and community work." [21] Empirical studies
related to the utilization of social research by social workers have
concentrated on opinions of research usage and on the extent to
which social workers say they have read research reports. Mc-
Culloch and Brown indicated that social workers in England
tended to read and publish in their own professional journals of
social work, rather than reading social science journals.[22] Rosenblatt conducted a survey of social caseworkers in which he
inquired about the extent to which they would read research articles to help determine a treatment plan for a difficult practice
case, and he reported that caseworkers valued personal consultation and supervision more than the reading of research articles.[23]
However, his study was concerned only with reading research as
opposed to personal contact with practice experts, who may have
had knowledge of research through either formal or informal
communication channels. Of interest in this regard is Eaton's
study of social workers in the Veterans Administration and the
California Department of Corrections in which he concluded
that 35 percent of those surveyed "ranked research first out of
five alternative organizational activities that would warrant expansion." (In addition to research, the alternatives included hiring psychiatric consultants, raising social work salaries, improving facilities for hospital and prison inmates, and raising salaries
for custodial personnel.) [24] Moreover, Eaton concluded that social workers in the Veterans Administration preferred verbal

channels over written channels for communicating research results about the ineffectiveness of their work. In fact, 86 percent of the 1,410 social workers queried "were quite willing to report research data verbally to their immediate supervisor, but less than half thought it wise to report the facts verbally at a special meeting of social workers, physicians, and nurses." [25]

In spite of these few illustrative studies, there is no available information about the actual amount of research utilized by practicing social workers. It is known, however, that schools of social work communicate information about social science theory and practice, much of which is based on social research. Furthermore, the amount of social work related research in the social sciences and in social work *per se* is increasing.[26]

In view of the need for social workers to incorporate useful research information, social work educators have focused on teaching students how to utilize research more effectively. Although there have been efforts to delineate criteria for the practitioner's use of research, sufficient models for utilization have yet to be developed.[27] This may be due to the fact that the burden for utilization has been placed primarily on social work practitioners, rather than on *both* researchers and practitioners.

The utilization of research information is dependent upon faithful communication from researchers to practitioners. In the communication process, knowledge produced by researchers is sent through various communication media, and social workers must receive that information before they can decide on its possible use and implementation. If the information is not adequately transmitted, i.e., if it is distorted before or after it is received, the likelihood of abusing, or ineffectively using, that information is increased. In this regard, then, the purpose of this book is to facilitate the process of research communication in social work by indicating how the transmission and reception of social research information might be effectively used, rather than abused. Toward this end, it is important to have a basic understanding of the process of social research and of some of the procedures that social researchers use to develop knowledge.

The Process of Social Research

Books on research typically indicate generalized principles pertaining to the conduct of research under idealized circumstances. The research process is generally conceived as including the following ingredients: the selection and formulation of a problem for research; the consideration of a research design, or logical strategy, to answer questions posed in the problem formulation; the selection of techniques for securing research observations; the processing and analyzing of data in relation to research hypotheses; and, finally, the conclusions and interpretations of the research.[28] Although the preceding aspects are included in most research studies, it is impossible to specify their precise relationship, other than to say that they are interrelated. In view of this, Bachrach enunciated his law about the planning and conduct of social research: [29] "People don't usually do research the way people who write books about research say that people do research."

Researchers do not do research as if it is based on a textbook scenario, simply because social researchers cannot plan and conduct research in a vacuum. Their research decisions are influenced by community sanctions, professional norms, ethics, research sponsors, the extent to which institutions and persons desire to participate in the research, and so forth. To illustrate the process of planning social research, here is an account of a hypothetical research study. It is concerned with the rehabilitation and treatment of youthful offenders, and is derived from my experiences as a research analyst.[30]

Over a decade ago two researchers were drinking coffee during a coffee-break and talking about such things as movies, civil rights, and theater. In the course of their conversation one researcher reported his impressions from a study in which he interviewed delinquent boys sent to training schools. One boy had been sent to a training school because he forged checks. When that boy was asked what he learned at the training school, he indicated that he acquired from his fellow inmates skills which would enable him to be more successful in forgery. This led both researchers to speculate that boys who are sent to training schools may learn more about techniques of crime than about how to keep out of trouble. They also identified some additional concerns which periodically came to the attention of their department, which was devoted to the rehabilitation and treatment of delinquent youths:

1. There are not enough institutions to adequately care for delinquent youths.
2. The state is faced with the problem of absorbing costs for building additional facilities.
3. Approximately one half of those boys released from state training schools violate the conditions of their parole within one year of release.

Given that information and faced with the reality that the coffee-break was over, the researchers went back to their work on different research projects. But they decided to continue the conversation the next day. In their subsequent discussion, they concluded somewhat facetiously that if institutions are costly and unsuccessful, they should be abolished. After having had a good laugh, they realized that that particular proposal was too simplistic and would probably not be adopted in any event. Then they began to discuss alternatives to institutionalization as more effective means for rehabilitation and as ways to deal with overcrowding. Influenced by their backgrounds in sociology and social work, they believed that it made good sense to treat delinquent youths in their own communities, rather than send them away to training schools. However, they could not specify what treatment in the community would consist of, and they were not aware of existing knowledge pertinent to this problem. Therefore, they decided to review the literature in this field.

They perused professional journals in social work, psychology, sociology, crime and delinquency, and found much speculation but little empirical evidence regarding their proposition that treatment of youthful offenders in the community is preferable to incarceration in a training school. A consistent observation was that youthful offenders had to adjust to the institution while there, and then readjust to the community in which they had got into trouble—a readjustment for which they were not adequately prepared.

The researchers spoke informally with several persons responsible for the treatment of delinquents in their state. It was noted that the costs incurred in the treatment of youthful offenders were regarded as excessive, and that legislators would prefer a treatment program that was cheaper than the existing one. There was also some speculation that the costs for community treatment might be considerably less than those for institutional treatment.

As a result of that process, the researchers formulated two related hypotheses:

1. Youthful offenders who receive treatment in their own community are less likely to recidivate (get into trouble again) than are those who are incarcerated at a training school and then released to the community.
2. The costs of community treatment will be significantly lower than the costs of institutional treatment.

The researchers, in essence, were experiencing a process of problem formulation in which they identified a problem for research and delimited tentative hypotheses. Their next step was to develop a research proposal which would include a research strategy and the kinds of data that could be gathered in relation to those hypotheses.

The strategy of experimentation was proposed. Youthful offenders, who normally would have been sent to a training school, would be randomly assigned either to institutional treatment or to treatment in the community. In addition, both groups of youthful offenders would be matched on the variables of sex, age, number of previous offenses, and types of offenses—variables which were related to recidivism as indicated by the statistical records of the research department where the researchers worked. The purpose of the random assignment and matching procedures was to provide for some degree of equivalence among the two groups of offenders. For example, if younger males were less likely to recidivate than older males, then both groups (institutional treatment and community treatment) should have contained similar proportions of younger and older males.

The researchers were concerned about sampling problems. Should all of the offenders in the state be included in the research, or should a sample of offenders be selected? The researchers believed that it might not be practicable to handle large numbers of youthful offenders in the beginning stages of a community treatment program, particularly with delinquent youth coming from many communities throughout the state. Therefore, they decided that the research should be conducted initially in one community, a community sending a large number of youthful offenders to training schools.

The researchers also had to consider which variables would reflect successful rehabilitation and how those variables could be measured, so that systematic comparisons could be made between the two groups in the experiment. They suggested variables such as the number of police contacts, the number of adjudicated offenses, the length of time youthful offenders stayed out of trouble after their rehabilitation experiences in either of the treatment programs, community adjustment as reflected in school attendance and in obtaining and maintaining jobs, evaluations of parents, and so forth. In addition, financial costs, manpower, and time to provide necessary services in the treatment programs were specified as variables.

Having delineated the major variables, the researchers then had to think of practical considerations related to the treatment program and the collection of data in the research. They discussed questions such as the following: How large should the community treatment staff be? Where in the community would such a project be located? How would the data be collected so that they would be relatively free of bias? Are there available techniques for quantifying the data so that comparisons could be made? How often and by whom would the data be collected? How would the data be analyzed? The researchers dealt with those questions as adequately as they could in developing their tentative research proposal. They could not answer many practical questions pertaining to the conduct of the research, because such questions can only be answered in the social context of the actual study. Therefore, they were ready to submit their proposal for criticisms and suggestions for revision to two different groups, one comprised of researchers and another comprised of administrators of rehabilitation and treatment programs in the state.

The group of researchers spotted several problems in the proposal. One problem was whether the proposal would be acceptable to *any* community. The proposal called for an early release of youthful offenders to a community, irrespective of their offenses. Judges and other community decision-makers might not allow offenders with such offenses as armed robbery, forcible rape, kidnapping, or assault with a deadly weapon, to remain in the community. Thus, it was believed that the sample of youthful offenders in the research program might have to be delimited more narrowly; for example, to include only those youths who were first offenders with less serious crimes. Most important, it was pointed out that the proposal would have to be developed in accordance with what the selected community would sanction, as well as with what the administrators of the treatment and rehabilitation facilities would allow.

A second major problem pointed out by the research staff was that the proposal did not specify the content of the community treatment program other than to indicate that group and individual counseling by professional social workers and psychologists would be conducted for each offender from two to three times per week, and that the offender would live either in his own home or in a foster home. The difficulty was that comparisons would not be meaningful if the researchers did not, in fact, know what was being compared. Therefore, it was suggested that the community treatment aspect of the proposal be developed further in conjunction with professional treatment persons.

Other problems with the technical aspects of the research were raised. For example, should the research design contain a control group which would receive no treatment? The researchers discussed whether it was ethical to deny treatment to youthful offenders, or to offer treatment that might not be successful. They concurred that it was both ethical and sufficient for their research purposes to compare two different treatment groups. After several meetings concerning the proposal, the research staff agreed that it was worthy of further development, but should first receive an endorsement from state administrators.

The two researchers revised their proposal to incorporate the suggestions made by the research staff. They decided that it would have been premature to detail the content of a community treatment program at that stage in the process, although they indicated in their revised proposal that it should be specified more completely, particularly in relation to program content and costs.

A meeting was then held with high level program administrators, who expressed interest in the idea that an alternative to institutional treatment might lead to a reduction in costs. Their major criticisms of the research proposal were similar to those of the research staff: the costs necessary to operate a community treatment program, including manpower and physical facilities, should be specified; and only first offenders with less serious offenses should be included as subjects in the experimental program.

A major concern of the administrators was that of financing the research project. They could arrange for some financing, but they doubted that they could defray the total costs of the project. The meeting concluded with an agreement that an additional researcher be hired to select a site where a community treatment project could be located; to determine whether it would be sanctioned by judges, the police, and other important community members; to develop a community treatment program; and to formulate the proposal in detail in order to submit it to a potential sponsor, such as the National Institute of Mental Health, for possible funding. The two researchers who initially submitted the proposal had other research obligations for their department, and they agreed that it would be desirable to hire a person who was expert in devising treatment programs and research designs to test those programs.

Within a few months an additional researcher was hired. The department was fortunate in finding a person with the qualifications desired. The researcher reviewed statistical records in order to locate communities where there were large numbers of first offenders, interviewed a variety of people in those communities about the feasibility of the research, interviewed and had meetings with the treatment staff in the department, had further discussions with administrators and treatment staff, and finally developed a research proposal which was submitted to the National Institute of Mental Health, and which was subsequently funded.

Once the funds were secured, the program was initiated on a pilot basis in order to determine whether it could be implemented. The plan was to conduct an experiment which involved random assignment of 200 male and female first offenders from the same community to either institutional or community treatment. The youths assigned to the community treatment program would receive individual and group counseling from one to three days per week. Counseling would include discussion of family and individual adjustment problems, educational planning, vocational guidance, and assistance with financial and other problems that might arise with individual youths and their families. The community treatment program would be housed in one small building, which would be leased on a yearly basis, and the community treatment staff would be comprised of ten persons experienced in the treatment of delinquent youth. Comparisons of the youth in the two treatment programs were to be made on such variables as police contacts, parole violations, and social adjustment.

As illustrated above, the process of initiating research can be complex. Researchers interact with a variety of people, and they usually make decisions about the conduct of research which are compromises between ideal research strategies and the practical constraints imposed by the social environment.

SOCIAL RESEARCH STRATEGIES

Social research is the systematic application of logical strategies and observational techniques for purposes of developing, modifying, and expanding knowledge about social phenomena.[31] In the preceding example, the purpose of the research was to test hypotheses regarding the relative efficiency and efficacy of institutional as opposed to community treatment. The strategy of experimentation was applied, and data gathered in the research were based on observations secured through police and court records, records of employment and school attendance, ratings of social adjustment, questionnaires, interviews, psychological tests, and records of financial costs and staff activities involved in the treatment programs.

There are three major strategies employed by social researchers in the study of social phenomena: experimentation, survey, and case study.[32]

Experimentation

The strategy of experimentation is employed to provide evidence related to causal assertions of the type, "If x . . . , then y." The variable x is regarded as a causal, independent, or experimental variable, while y is designated as an effect or dependent variable. Evidence that is necessary for testing such an assertion is that x and y are related, that x occurs prior in time to y, and that variables other than x are not responsible for the observed changes in y.[33] For example, to test the assertion that psychotherapy (x) for anxious persons leads to a reduction in anxiety (y), it must be shown that: 1) there is, in fact, a reduction of anxiety that is related to the provision of psychotherapy; 2) the reduction in anxiety occurs after the introduction of psychotherapy; and 3) other variables, such as the receipt of tranquilizing drugs, are not responsible for the observed reduction in anxiety.

Experimentation contains the following ingredients: manipulation of experimental variables, the provision of control groups, procedures for equating experimental and control groups, and the inclusion of variables which can be reliably measured and are amenable to statistical analysis.[34]

A variable can be manipulated by specifying the conditions under which it would occur and by arranging for its exposure to research subjects. For example, psychotherapy may be identified as a form of treatment based on verbal interactions between psychotherapists and their clients. It may be manipulated by deciding in advance of the research whether or not persons will receive psychotherapy and what its amount and duration will be. Thus, anxious persons could be assigned to experimental or treatment groups where the duration, amount, and type of psychotherapy would be specified.

Control groups are employed to answer the question: would changes in y occur without the introduction of x? Would an anxious person be relieved of his anxiety (y) as a result of the passage of time (without x)? The strategy is to assign persons similar to those in an experimental group (which receives x) to a control group (which does not receive x) so that comparisons can be made on changes in y. If anxiety is reduced when psychotherapy is provided *and* if it is not reduced when psychotherapy is not provided, then it is plausible to infer that psychotherapy leads to a reduction in anxiety.

In order to rule out the potential influence of other variables on y, procedures are employed to provide for comparable groups of persons in experimental and control groups.[35] One device is simply to define the research population so that persons are similar on other variables that could influence y.

For example, persons who are "older" might be less anxious than persons who are "younger," i.e., there might be a relationship between age and anxiety. By defining as subjects for the research only those persons who are "younger" (or "older"), the population is made more comparable on the variable of age. It is apparent, however, that this procedure would restrict the extent to which one would generalize the results of the research, i.e., if younger persons are studied, the results could not be generalized to older persons. Another procedure used to rule out the influence of age is "matching." For each person in the experimental group who is "old," there would be a person in the control group who is also "old"; correspondingly, for each person in the experimental group who is "young," there would be a matching "young" person in the control group. Still another procedure would be to balance the frequency distributions on age in the experimental and control groups. If the experimental group is comprised of 60 percent "old" persons and 40 percent "young" persons, then the control group would have the same distribution (60 percent "old," 40 percent "young") as the experimental group.

These procedures are advantageous if the researcher knows which variables, other than x, are related to y prior to the execution of an experiment. However, there may be still other variables that relate to y, but the researcher may not be aware of them. In this instance, the device of randomization is desirable, for it is that procedure which is most likely to produce similar distributions on a large number of variables for the experimental and control groups. Research subjects are assigned by a random process either to an experimental or to a control group. For example, an anxious person may be assigned to an experimental group when a coin tossed in the air lands as "heads," or to a control group when the coin lands as "tails."

Experimentation must include variables that can be measured reliably. This means that under the same conditions of measurement that independent investigators would make the same observations. For example, suppose that the concept of anxiety is defined operationally as the number of sentences, in a 50-sentence "test" of symptoms of anxiety, that a person indicates are descriptive of how he feels; the higher the number, the higher the anxiety. If the anxiety scores would fluctuate upon retesting under the same test conditions, the measure would be unreliable. On the contrary, if two or more independent researchers test the same person on different days and obtain identical results, the measure of anxiety could be regarded as reliable. In addition, the measure should be a valid reflection of the concept of anxiety. The contents of the sentences should relate to conceptions of anxiety, and the test should distinguish between persons judged as high or low in anxiety on other measures such as psychiatric ratings or physiological indications of anxiety.

The stragegy of experimentation presented here is that of the "classical experimental research design," where subjects are randomly assigned to experimental or control groups, and measurements are obtained on the dependent variable prior to and subsequent to the exposure of the independent variable. This is a basic experimental design, and it is used for evaluating social programs as well as for testing causal hypotheses pertaining to the effectiveness of techniques related to social work interventions.[36] It is an ideal model and is subject to variations, which are dictated by the complexity of the research hypotheses and the social context in which the research takes place.

One major variation is that of multivariate experimental design where multiple independent and dependent variables are investigated simultaneously.[37] An experiment may be devised to test for the joint relationship between types of psychotherapy (individual or group therapy) and duration of treatment (six weeks or six months) on the reduction of anxiety and the increase in job satisfaction. Highly anxious subjects might be randomly assigned to one of five groups: individual therapy for six weeks, individual therapy for six months, group therapy for six weeks, group therapy for six months, or a control group with no therapy. Prior to the introduction of the treatments in the various groups, all research subjects would be measured on the variables of anxiety and job satisfaction. In addition, repeated measurements on those variables might be obtained at durations of six weeks, six months, and one year.

A second major variation in experimental designs has to do with the formation of quasi-experiments, i.e., research studies devised to test causal assertions but which cannot utilize all of the procedures included in experimentation.[38] The strategy is that of approximating ideal experimental design. For example, if it is not possible to use randomization, a contrast group may be used as an approximation to a control group. The experimental group might be comprised of clients who are male executives between the ages of 25 and 40 years, highly anxious, and desirous of psychotherapy. All of those persons would receive psychotherapy. For a contrast group, the researcher may locate another group of executives who are similar to those assigned to the experimental group but who did not seek psychotherapy. The groups are similar, but they are not as equivalent as they would be if randomization were employed for all those executives seeking therapy. Measurements would be taken, and comparisons would be made between the experimental and contrast groups.

Survey

There are two major purposes of survey methods: description and explanation.[39] For its descriptive function, the strategy of surveys includes procedures for obtaining representative samples, describing frequency distributions within variables and quantitative relationships among variables, describing trends over time and, as in experimentation, specifying variables which can be reliably measured.

In a survey which attempts to describe the opinions of Michigan residents about the use of busing to integrate public schools, several procedures might be employed. The population to which the researchers wish to generalize is defined. It could be all residents in the state of Michigan, or it might be limited to those adult residents of the state who have children enrolled in public schools.

Because it may be too costly and time consuming to obtain opinions from every person in the designated study population, researchers may employ sampling methods. The logic involved is that the opinions of the population can be inferred from a sample if the sample is representative of that population. To obtain a representative sample, any of a combination of procedures such as area sampling, cluster sampling, and stratified random sampling could be used.[40] One sampling plan would be to use the state's division into counties, selecting two counties with the largest populations, and then randomly selecting four of the remaining, listed counties. Second, one might divide the public schools within each county by their designations as high school, junior high school, or elementary school. Within each of the chosen six counties, two schools of each type might be randomly selected. Third, lists of parents of children attending each of the 36 schools (six counties times six schools in each county) would be obtained. From each of the 36 lists the names of 50 adults would be randomly drawn. In selecting a random sample, all elements of the population are listed; then a random process, such as a lottery or a table of random numbers, is used to choose a specified number of elements. Each element of the population has the same chance of being included in the sample. For example, 50 adults might have been selected from one school which has a population of 1,000 adults; each of the 1,000 adults (or elements) would have had the same chance of being included in the random sample.

Having chosen a sample, the survey researcher attempts to obtain the cooperation of respondents to participate in the survey, then he compiles observations based on such devices as questionnaires and interviews. Since there would be 1,800 persons in the hypothetical survey above (36 schools times 50 persons in each school), it would be necessary to have a staff of interviewers trained in eliciting reliable responses from the interviewees. Thus, the researchers would have to specify the types of questions that the interviewers would ask. There may be questions about the ethnic identity of the respondents as well as questions about whether they are in favor of or opposed to busing as a means to achieve integration. Considerable thought would go into the construction of the interview schedule so that reliable data could be gathered relatively free from the biases of the interviewers.

When the interviews are completed, the responses are coded so that they can be processed and analyzed with the aid of electronic computers. The results of such a study might be that 40 percent of the respondents are in favor of busing, 40 percent are opposed, 10 percent have no opinion, and 10 percent refused to answer the question. In addition to describing the frequency distribution of respondents' preferences for busing, there may be descriptions of quantitative relationships among variables. For example, there might be a relationship between ethnic identity and busing preference. Blacks may be more in favor of busing than are whites, while whites may be more opposed to busing.

This type of survey, which is conducted at one point in time, is a cross-sectional survey.[41] In addition to describing opinions at one point in time, survey researchers may use procedures for describing the same preferences over several points in time. One device is to repeat the survey, for example at yearly intervals, and then to compare the results to indicate whether there appear to be changes in preferences for or against busing. This can be done by taking different samples of subjects (repeated cross-sectional studies) or by using the same sample of subjects for repeated interviewing (panel design).[42]

Descriptive surveys are used to provide descriptions of opinions, needs of the clientele of social agencies, the extent to which people use existing health services, and so forth. They can include a variety of questions about many social phenomena and, because of this, they are often characterized as providing extensive information.[43] However, the information is usually derived from responses to a few questions, and it typically does not include detailed considerations of why respondents answer the survey questions the way they do.

The explanatory purpose of surveys includes the same strategies as involved in description, as well as the following procedures: the comparison of contrasting populations, and the use of data analytic methods for determining relationships among variables and for making inferences about causal relationships.

The correlational or comparative study is used to make inferences about two or more contrasting populations.[44] For example, a representative sample might be obtained from a population characterized as those persons who received money from public welfare for one year but who are now currently employed and off the "welfare rolls." Another sample may be drawn from a contrasting population which might be comprised of those persons who have been receiving welfare benefits for more than one year and who are still on the "welfare rolls." Persons in each sample might be asked a number of questions about their life circumstances, job skills, availability of jobs in the area, physical handicaps, etc. The purpose of such a study would be to seek those variables related to the necessity for continued subsistence from public welfare. In the analyses of data the plan might be to first locate variables that distinguish between the two groups. Those who continue on welfare may be white, while persons who do not continue may be black. Second, the researchers might analyze that relationship with respect to other variables. Would there still be a relationship between ethnic identity and continuance on welfare, when education is statistically controlled? It might be found that there is a higher correlation between education and welfare continuance than between ethnic identity and welfare continuance. By analyzing the relationship of ethnic identity to welfare continuance separately for those with low and high educational achievement, it might be observed that the relationship is no longer maintained.

The panel design might also be used in conjunction with the comparative design in that two contrasting populations can be studied over time with respect to their experiences related to the phenomenon under study. Do the respondents go on and off the "welfare rolls," for what reasons, and under what circumtances? Information could be gathered and manipulated in data analyses to determine whether the same relationships are maintained or are influenced by other variables over varying points in time.

When researchers use surveys to explain relationships among variables and to make inferences about causality, they often use procedures such as those indicated above. In addition, they may attempt to approximate some of the procedures used in experimentation. Although surveys typically include more representative sampling than do experiments, they lack the degree of internal control provided in experiments by such methods as variable manipulation and randomization. Thus, although the survey researcher can attempt to estimate the time order of other variables on a dependent variable, it is virtually impossible to do so with a high degree of certainty. The logic of the approach is to rule out as many variables as possible and to make inferences about causality on the basis of the data that can be gathered. On the other hand, when the purpose of a survey is to provide descriptions of a large population on a few variables, it is both an economical and a relatively precise strategy.

Case Study

The basic strategy of a case study is to thoroughly describe a single unit—an individual, a group, an organization, a community—for the purposes of developing ideas for subsequent investigations, clarifying concepts, and formulating hypotheses. Case studies can be used to describe such diverse phenomena as the organization of a mental hospital, the decision-making structure of communities, the formation and dissolution of political groups, the actions of a neighborhood in relation to urban renewal, and the behavioral changes of a client undergoing stressful situations.[45]

Although the logical strategy of case studies is less subject to codification than those of experimentation and survey methods, there are several features which can be identified: the description of past history through available sources of information, the description of a phenomenon over time by gathering a wide variety of quantitative and qualitative data, the selection of instances of contrasting experiences, and the flexible role of the researcher in integrating and summarizing his observations.

The purpose of describing the history of a unit (e.g., an organization) is to place observations of the present in the context of the past. For example, a researcher may be interested in studying decisions made about mental patients in a public psychiatric hospital, and he may raise a series of questions. What kinds of treatment do patients receive? How are they treated by ward attendants? When and under what conditions are they released? The researcher might talk with hospital executives about the purpose and functions of the hospital. He also may ask about the hospital's history, and whether there are records which pertain to it.

Records of policy statements, executive committee meetings, ward observations, patients' progress, annual progress reports, etc., may be available. The researcher may read selectively from those sources to obtain a picture of major changes that have occurred, such as differences in hiring practices, turnover in personnel, and increases or decreases in the amount of time that patients stay in the hospital. In particular, the researcher may look for unusual circumstances which may affect the present. The previous hospital administrator may have been regarded as "weak" in that he did not have a sufficient degree of control. This information may be gleaned from hospital documents, newspaper articles reporting on the event, and from staff members and patients who were in the hospital when the previous administrator was there. Such information may help to explain the attitudes of the current administrator, who may be constrained to maintain a high degree of control.

A second procedure employed in case studies is to describe the current structure and organization of the unit and then to observe it over time.[46] The administrative structure and organization of the hospital may be described with respect to various functions and roles of the staff and activities of the patients. There may be weekly staff meetings pertaining to patient and staff needs and memoranda regarding hospital practices and policies. The contents of those documents may contain decisions that affect the patients. Records also may be kept on medication, other treatments that patients receive, and progress in hospital jobs and activity groups. The researcher learns what information is routinely collected so that he can refer to it as he becomes immersed in his study. But, inevitably, he selects some unit of observation that pertains to his interest.

It would be impossible to observe simultaneously all of the patients in the hospital, so the investigator may focus his inquiry on one ward of patients. He might be interested in how patients are assigned to the ward and who makes decisions about them. To study this phenomenon, he may interview staff and patients on the ward in relation to their daily activities, and he may observe interactions among staff and patients as they occur throughout a hospital day. He might record interviews, write down his impressions, and observe the number and type of interactions that take place in relation to patients' requests for privileges. The purpose of gathering a wide range of information is to describe the phenomenon in detail and to provide a context for generating ideas. In this process, the researcher may narrow his interests, discarding some types of data and adding others. For example, he may observe that ward attendants vary in the ways in which they respond to patients. Some attendants automatically deny all requests, while others are more permissive. Hence, the investigator may focus on decisions made by ward attendants and attempt to locate variables that might influence those decisions.

To investigate this phenomenon more thoroughly, the researcher might use a third procedure, that of selecting contrasting experiences.[47] The ward he observed may have contained only patients regarded as ready for discharge, i.e., they may have been less disturbed than other patients in the hospital. In view of this, the investigator may choose a contrasting group of patients, those who are regarded as being more severely ill and who have been in the hospital for a number of years. Patients of that type may be confined to another ward, and the researcher may decide to observe whether or not different ward attendants also vary in their responses to those patients. The strategy is to obtain observations on the contrasting groups in order to formulate hypotheses about the behavior of ward attendants. There too, the researcher may find that ward attendants vary. He then looks for similarities and differences among the ward attendants and attempts to relate that information to their response patterns to patients. For example, ward attendants with less education may be more restrictive, while those with more education may be relatively permissive in granting patients' requests, irrespective of the type of patient encountered.

Finally, the investigator integrates his previous theoretical predispositions and his perceptions of the various kinds of data he gathered in order to describe the hospital ward and the ways in which patients are affected by decisions. This process allows for a great deal of flexibility on the part of the researcher. It is imprecise for making factual generalizations since the biases of the researcher are not controlled.[48] However, it allows him to formulate hypotheses which may lead to advances in knowledge. For example, the researcher may have speculated that higher levels of education may lead to more tolerant attitudes toward the mentally ill, and that is why ward attendants differ in the extent to which they grant patients' requests.

The case study method can be combined with experimental or survey methods in the investigation of social phenomena. For example, a demonstration project may have the purpose of determining the feasibility of providing new services to a clientele group. The services may be experimentally manipulated, and detailed observations of the clients' experiences, attitudes, and behavioral changes may be described.[49] Similarly, in clinical drug trials a new drug is prescribed and detailed observations may be made to determine whether desirable changes are produced and whether undesirable side effects are absent. Moreover, surveys may be combined with a case study of selected community leaders in order to describe attitudinal changes regarding such issues as urban renewal.

OBSERVATIONAL TECHNIQUES

Observational techniques are used to gather the data that are processed and analyzed in social research. Although there are a variety of such techniques, they can be classified by two major dimensions: the sources of data and the structure of data.[50]

Sources of Data

Primary data sources are those data directly gathered by researchers. There are two types of observational techniques. One type includes direct questioning by the researcher, i.e., questionnaires, interviews, and tests; while a second type consists of techniques which do not primarily involve direct questioning by the researcher, such as live observations, ratings, and the use of mechanical devices.

A questionnaire contains a series of written questions to be an-

swered by the research subject and then returned to the researcher.[51] It requires that the respondent be able to read and
write, and that he is interested enough in the questions to answer
them. The questions are devised by the researcher and pertain to
variables considered necessary for his research. For example,
there may be questions about the respondent's age, marital status,
income, and his opinions about the desirability of socialized medical and health services. The technique is advantageous in
quickly securing information from a large number of people, particularly highly educated persons who are willing to answer the
questions and return the questionnaires. However, there is
usually an incomplete return rate, and respondents may be less
prone to answer questions of a personal nature than they would in
face-to-face interviews with the researcher.

An interview is an encounter in which the researcher seeks the
cooperation of a respondent in answering a series of questions.[52]
The researcher obtains answers to those questions, and he also
has the opportunity to clarify the respondent's answers and to
make judgments about the accuracy of those responses. The interview is advantageous in that it can be used with a variety of
people who are more likely to respond to personal than to imper-
sonal inquiry, as in questionnaires. However, the answers to interview questions can be influenced by characteristics of the in-
terviewer and the setting in which the interview takes place.
This is why interviewers are trained to maintain relatively neu-
tral postures and to show consistent attitudes and styles in eliciting responses from research subjects.

Tests are similar to questionnaires in that a series of questions
are presented for the respondents to answer. Whereas questionnaires usually aim to elicit information about the respondents'
perceptions and opinions of social phenomena, tests are devised
to determine whether research subjects can answer questions
correctly. For example, an achievement test in reading may be
administered to all of the students in a junior high school. The
test might contain paragraphs to be read, followed by a number
of questions devised to test the accuracy of each respondent's
reading comprehension. Average rates of accuracy may be computed for the junior high school students, and their reading com-

prehension scores may be compared with those of students from other schools.

There are a variety of tests—intelligence tests, achievement tests, aptitude tests, etc.[53] They are especially useful when the researcher is interested in describing how different groups of people perform on them. However, tests may be disadvantageous if norms of performance are not available, or if they are administered to populations different from the populations for which they were originally constructed. For example, if the content of paragraphs in a reading comprehension test is based on the material that an upper middle-class population reads, e.g., *Harpers*, as opposed to the material read by a lower-class population, e.g., *Popular Mechanics*, the test may be prejudicial in favor of upper middle-class respondents.

An observational technique which is not based primarily on direct questioning is that of live observation. The researcher observes behavior as it occurs, and he records his observations. For example, he may observe the behavior of infants in a pediatric ward and record the frequency of crying, length of time for eating, and so on. Or, the researcher may observe a parole board deciding on whether or not parole should be granted to those who request it; and he may record the number of different themes that are brought into discussion, his impressions of who the most influential board members are, etc.

Depending on his relationship to the persons observed, the researcher may be engaged in nonparticipant or participant observation.[54] In nonparticipant observation, the observer does not interact with the subjects of his inquiry. Thus, the observer may attend meetings of a parole board, but not take part in its discussions. In some situations, he might observe individuals or groups with the aid of a one-way mirror—where the researcher can see the research subjects, but they cannot see him.

Participant observation is a technique in which the researcher observes while he participates. For example, in observing a group of citizens who are formulating plans for urban renewal, the observer may become acquainted with the individual members of the group and engage in discussions with the group about their proposals to a city council. Participant observation has been used widely by anthropologists and sociologists to study diverse phenomena such as the formation of delinquent gangs and the rituals that take place in different societies and religions.[55]

Techniques of live observation are useful when subjects are not able to respond to questions (e.g., infants) or when they do not wish to respond. Moreover, information can be gathered about a phenomenon as it occurs, rather than after the fact through questions which depend on the accurate recall of respondents. The chief disadvantage of participant observation is that it is difficult to rule out the effects of bias in the observations that the researcher chooses to record. In addition, the phenomenon that is being observed may change simply as a function of the presence of the observer—i.e., what the observer observes may be due to his presence, which alters the natural situation. On the other hand, participant observation may be the only way to gain access to a group one wants to study, and it may furnish the investigator with a number of insights he could not have gained through other means. Of utmost importance in live observation are the decisions about what is to be observed and how the observations are to be recorded, whether by simple narrative description or by other techniques such as rating scales and mechanical devices.

A rating scale is a device by which an observer (or a "judge") rates the extent to which the person or object observed can be characterized by one of an ordered series of categories.[56] For example, a researcher may be interested in observing the amount of social contact a psychiatric patient has with other patients on a hospital ward. A rating scale of social contact may take the following form: [57]

1	2	3	4	5
Very hostile to other patients or always by himself.	Shows interest when approached by other patients but rarely talks to them.	Usually tries to be around other patients but is passive socially.	Spends some time with one or two patients.	Spends considerable time with patients.

After having observed the patient on the ward during different portions of a day, the researcher chooses that category (1 through 5) which is most descriptive of the patient's social contacts.

A series of rating scales may be used to judge a variety of behaviors. The ratings might be made by researchers, or they could be made by other persons who have observed the behaviors in question. For example, a patient's social contacts in a psychiatric ward could be rated by a social worker, a psychiatric nurse, a ward attendant, or even the patient himself. The chief advantages of rating scales are that they provide economical ways of observing behavior, and behaviors of more than one person can be compared for purposes of description or as variables for testing hypotheses. However, rating scales impose an arbitrary ordering of behavior, and independent observers may not be able to agree on their ratings of the same phenomenon. Thus, researchers who use rating scales must provide satisfactory answers to questions such as the following: do the points of the scale make sense, i.e., do they relate to the variable of interest? who should make the ratings? will the judgments be free of bias? how much information is necessary to make sound judgments? [58]

To facilitate the recording of information mechanical devices such as movie cameras and tape recorders may be used. The primary virtue of using movies and tape recordings is that the event being studied is preserved. Mechanical devices are less subject to recording errors, and they provide data which can be used for many research purposes. Watches can be used to record amounts of time spent in job activities, special instruments can be used to record the level of noise in a classroom, weighing scales can be used to record weight gain or loss, and so on. Of course, the use of those devices is costly, and their presence in an observational setting may alter the natural behavior of those observed. Moreover, it may be extremely difficult to summarize and process the vast amounts of information acquired.

Secondary data sources refer to those data used by researchers but not collected by them.[59] Secondary data may include sources such as stored data obtained from research, documents, products of communication media, and statistical information. All of these

sources contain available data which have been collected, typically, for purposes different than those of the research investigator. If the data can be adapted for the researcher's use, they are
extremely valuable. Time and money may be conserved, and the
data may be more extensive than the researcher could obtain
through primary data collection techniques.

Stored data obtained from research is data gathered by such
techniques as questionnaires or observations in a previous research study which are available for the researcher's use. For example, a public opinion survey may have been conducted on the
preferences of community residents for designated political candidates. During that survey a great deal of additional information
may have been secured about income, number of persons living
in a household, ethnic identity, etc. A researcher may be interested in the relationship between ethnic identity and housing
conditions. If the information from the previous survey is sufficient for his purpose and if he has access to the data, then he may
analyze those data for his research, a procedure referred to as secondary analysis.[60] Data which can be used for secondary analyses
are stored in a number of institutions in the United States, such as
the Yale Economic Growth Center, the National Opinion Research Center, and the International Development Bank.* These
institutions maintain data on numerous social phenomena ranging from information on the economic development of countries
throughout the world to legislative records of public officials.

Another source of data for research is that of available documents.[61] Documents include minutes of meetings, recordings of
casework interviews, logs or descriptive accounts of community
organization workers, personal diaries, biographies, marriage
certificates, legal papers, and so forth. When the information is
regarded as accurate, it can be used for descriptive purposes in
narrative form, or it can be converted for use on rating scales. For
example, the logs of community organizers may contain descriptions of their daily activities. A researcher may rate those com-

* Data stored in research institutes and other facilities are often referred to as
data banks. The accessibility and retrieval of data from data banks are important
requisites for secondary data analyses.

munity organizers with respect to the amount of time spent with professionals in existing social agencies as compared to the amount of time spent with nonprofessionals in order to distinguish among different types of community organizers. Although many kinds of documents are available, they may not be useful for research. The specific information the researcher requires may not have been recorded systematically, and different recorders may have emphasized different types of information and may have varied in their accuracy of recording.

Related to documents as a source of data are the contributions of communication media such as newspapers, television, radio, and films. While these contributions have the same disadvantages as do documents, they can be useful for reporting events that take place in the environment, for describing that information which has been made public and which could influence persons in a community, and for reviewing issues that appeared to have been of importance in the past. For example, editorials and articles on social welfare programs, as well as the amount of space and time devoted by the media to such programs, may be indicative, indirectly, of the public's attitude toward social welfare. Of course, those who prepare the transmissions may not be representative of the public, and the researcher may resort to direct questioning of the populace. However, he may combine information from the media with his interviews, for example, to determine the extent to which public attitudes are shaped or reinforced by the communications media.

A final source of secondary data is that of statistical records: records and statistics of national and local censuses, statistics describing the numbers and types of clients in social agencies, vital statistics regarding birth and death rates, indices of unemployment, records of persons who appear in court, descriptions of the lengths of time that persons spend in various institutions.[62] Such records are extremely useful in research. They may serve as basic variables in a research study, or they may provide information for determining the extent to which a sample is representative of a population. For example, a sample of 1,000 residents in a community may be used to generalize to a population of 10,000 residents. If statistics describing characteristics of the population are available (such as age, sex, and income level), the researcher can check the extent to which his sample has characteristics similar to that of the population (i.e., same proportion of males, same age distribution, etc.). In using such statistics, however, the researcher must often assume that they are accurate. Errors may have been made in classification, tabulation, or the processing of records. When evidence of the soundness of the records is scanty, the researcher may choose to devise his own system of recording information, particularly if a great deal of accuracy is required in his study.

Structure of Data

A second major dimension for classifying observational techniques is that of structure. Structured data refers to the extent to which the research observations are recorded into categories which have been previously specified. Rating scales require that the observer chooses among several alternatives for recording his observations, and they are, therefore, structured observations. On the other hand, data obtained through the narrative descriptions of the researcher in participant observation are relatively unstructured, since precise categories of observation are not specified.

Primary data sources and secondary data sources may contain data which are either structured or unstructured. A structured questionnaire contains specific questions to which the respondent replies by selecting one or more of several predesignated alternatives.[63] For example, answers to the question: "Have you discussed your problems with a social worker in the past 30 days?" may be indicated as "no," "yes," "not applicable" (no problems). A structured questionnaire may be comprised of fixed-alternative questions as in the above example and / or a series of rating scales in which the respondent indicates the extent of his agreement with items, or sentences, representing certain attitudes. For example, "Indicate the extent to which you agree or disagree with the following statement [1 is strongly agree; 2 is agree; 3 is disagree; and 4 is strongly disagree]: People who receive welfare payments are basically lazy."

A questionnaire may include questions that do not have specified alternatives, i.e., unstructured questions. An example of such a question is: "What kinds of tasks do social workers perform on their jobs?" Respondents may answer this by saying they do not know, or by listing one activity, such as the investigation of welfare clients, or by listing a wide range of activities.

Interviews may include structured questions that are read to respondents, or they may be unstructured and consist of a series of questions which the researcher devises as the interview progresses. Data from live observations may also be structured or unstructured, whereas data from documents and the media are usually in an unstructured form—which can be converted to structured data by the use of rating scales or other devices, such as measurements of the amount of space in a newspaper devoted to a certain topic.

The primary advantage of structured data is that it is in a form which can lead to quantitative comparisons of the observations. Responses to the same fixed-alternative questions can be tabulated and compared quite easily. Unstructured data provide more flexibility in responses than structured data, and they contain information that could lead to fruitful hypotheses and ideas for subsequent research. However, unstructured data are more difficult to convert into a form for quantitative measurement, and comparisons may be difficult, if not impossible, to make.

THE QUANTIFICATION OF DATA

Before data can be appropriately used for quantitative comparisons, certain requirements must be met. Irrespective of the observational technique employed, the data should conform to a measurement scale, and the measurement scale should be reliable and valid. There are four commonly used measurement scales in social research: nominal, ordinal, interval, and ratio.[64] The nominal scale is comprised of two or more categories that are mutually exclusive and exhaustive. In a simple scale for classifying persons by sex, there are two categories, i.e., male and female. The categories are mutually exclusive, in that a person classified as a male can not also be classified as a female, and the categories are exhaustive, in that all people can be classified as being predominantly male or female. Thus, in describing 100 executives one might observe that 80 are male, while 20 are female.

An ordinal scale contains categories which have an ordered relationship and which are also mutually exclusive and exhaustive. For example, a rating scale regarding the amount of participation of individual members in a group may contain three categories: active participation, moderate participation, and no participation. The ordered relationship refers to the notion that active participation is more than moderate participation, which in turn is more than no participation. Although an ordinal scale represents "more than" or "less than" relations among categories, it does not indicate the precise degree of those relations. Two boys may be rank ordered by height into the categories of shortest and tallest; however, from that information it is obvious that the degree of difference between the heights of the two boys is unknown.

In addition to having the characteristics of nominal and ordinal scales (mutually exclusive and exhaustive categories; categories ordered into "more than" and "less than" relations), interval scales have the property of numerically equal distances between adjacent categories. For example, a thermometer provides measurements in degrees on an interval scale. A room which registers 100 degrees on a thermometer is one degree hotter than a room which registers 99 degrees, which, correspondingly, is one degree hotter than a room which registers 98 degrees.

A ratio scale has all the characteristics of an interval scale in addition to having a natural or absolute zero point that has empirical meaning. Whereas a scale of weight has such a zero point, a thermometer scale does not. Hence, while one could say that a person who weighs 50 pounds is half as heavy as one who weighs 100 pounds, he could not accurately make the assertion that a day with a recorded temperature of 100 degrees is twice as hot as a day in which the temperature is 50 degrees. This is because the measurement scale of weight is the only one of the two scales which has an absolute zero, and this allows for the above arithmetic operations to correspond with the properties of the scale, i.e., to make sense.

Transforming research observations into one of the levels of measurement is necessary in order to make quantitative comparisons. Furthermore, the type of quantitative comparisons that can be employed depend upon the level of measurement obtained. For example, percentages and proportions can be computed for all levels of measurement: medians, for ordinal, interval, and ratio scales; arithmetic means, for interval and ratio scales; and the geometric mean, for ratio scales.[65]

As indicated previously, reliability of measurement refers to the extent to which repeated application of measuring devices, under the same conditions of measurement, yield consistent results free from bias or error.[66] Although there are a variety of procedures for estimating the reliability of measurement scales, there are several types of reliability that are most frequently employed: test-retest, inter-judge agreement, and item equivalence.

Test-retest reliability is the consistency of measurement obtained when the same observational technique is used at two or more different points in time. In a reliable weighing scale, the scale would indicate the same weight for a person on two separate weighings in a five-minute time span. An interview schedule for assessing attitudes toward busing would be reliable if, in repeated applications of the interview in a relatively short time span such as one or two weeks, the same responses would be observed and recorded.

Inter-judge agreement is a type of reliability which indicates the extent to which two or more "judges" agree in their ratings, classifications, or judgments of the same phenomenon. If several researchers who code responses of unstructured questionnaires agree in their use of a system for classifying those responses, the system is considered to be reliable.

Finally, item equivalence refers to the extent to which responses on "equivalent forms" of the same test or instrument are consistent. For example, two questionnaires may have been devised to measure attitudes toward capital punishment. The items in each questionnaire are parallel in that they have the same content, but they are worded differently. Both questionnaires may be administered at the same time to a sample of respondents. To the extent that the responses to one questionnaire are similar to those on the other, the questionnaires are said to be reliable.

Reliabilities are typically expressed in correlations and percentage agreements. The greater the degree of correlation (.00 is no correlation, .50 is a moderate correlation, .85 is a high correlation, and 1.00 is a perfect correlation) or percentage agreement (from 0 to 100 percent), the higher is the degree of reliability.[67] High reliabilities are required to accurately describe quantitative relations among variables.

Validity refers to the extent of correspondence between the measurement of a variable and the intended meaning of that variable.[68] In other words, a valid measurement device is one which measures what we think it is supposed to measure. There are two general approaches for validating social measurements. One refers to the contents of the measurement scale, known as content validity; while another, predictive validity, is based on the extent to which predictions can be successfully made to other phenomena presumably related to the variable in question. Content validity is essentially the notion that the contents of a measurement device (e.g., the items in a test, or the questions in a questionnaire) should be conceptually related to what is being measured. A test devised to assess arithmetic skills should contain a sampling of items which are representative of typical uses of arithmetic, i.e., addition, subtraction, multiplication, division, fractions, decimals, etc. To achieve content validity for a classification scale which aims to distinguish among different types of community organizers, the classification scale should contain categories related to the various functions of community organizers.

Predictive validity involves a prediction from the variable being validated to another variable.[69] For example, a questionnaire devised to determine preferences for candidates in a political race is valid if the responses on the questionnaire are highly correlated with the actual votes cast. Predictions may also be made about the relationship of concurrent phenomena. The researcher's observations of withdrawn behavior of group members are valid if they are correlated with (or predictive of) the ratings of the group members themselves. Another kind of predictive validity is that of predicting responses for two contrasting groups—one which is judged to have the phenomenon in question, while the other does not. For example, two contrasting groups might be comprised of high school honor students in both citizenship and scholarship, on the one hand; and similarly aged students who have been adjudicated as juvenile delinquents and who are high school drop-outs, on the other hand. It might be reasoned that a questionnaire devised to test for attitudes toward delinquency should discriminate between these two groups, i.e., the honor students should be less likely to favor antisocial activities than the group of adjudicated delinquents. Hence, the questionnaire would be regarded as valid if adjudicated delinquents indicate that they are more predisposed to antisocial activities than are the honor students.

Thus, the research process involves a consideration of research strategies, observational techniques, and the quantification of data. The basic concepts which have been presented in this chapter are necessary for understanding the levels of knowledge that are produced in social research studies. In chapter 2, criteria will be presented for evaluating social research knowledge.

Chapter 2

~~~~~~

Knowledge from
Social Research

Social research has as its primary goal the development of knowledge about social phenomena. While some of this knowledge is directly related to the functions and activities of social workers, much of it is more relevant to the expansion and modification of social science concepts and theories—which ultimately may be applicable to social work endeavors. Because the profession of social work contains subdisciplines having different functions, it draws upon knowledge from a variety of sources such as the following: legal and medical facts and interpretations, experiences of practitioners who work in social agencies, information about agency policies and procedures, social science conceptual formulations, and findings of social research which bear on social work practice.

Types of Knowledge

Social work scholars have not provided an all-encompassing classification for assembling knowledge from social research that is applicable to the content of social work activity.[1] This is probably due to the eclecticism of social work and to the wide range of information that social work employs from other disciplines and professions. Nevertheless, several classification systems have been developed which are illustrative of types of social research knowledge pertinent to social work.

Greenwood devised a scheme for classifying research studies into operational social work research and basic social work research.[2] Operational social work research includes studies on immediate administrative and planning activities of social agencies, i.e., descriptive statistics, planning information and administrative information; while basic social work research includes studies on the history, philosophy, and culture of social work, measurement theory, and practice theory. The primary difficulty with this scheme is that the distinction between operational and basic research is difficult to apply. Moreover, there are no extensive theories which interrelate and explain facts about social work activities, and social work has traditionally incorporated theoretical conceptions—such as ego psychology, role theory, and behavior modification—from other disciplines. Thus, Greenwood's system is narrowly defined in that it does not allow for the systematic incorporation of social research knowledge from other disciplines.

A more general classification for organizing knowledge from social research is provided by Thomas, who employs two major dimensions for selecting knowledge that has content relevance for social work: subject matter and the level to which subject matter is applied.[3] The subject matter is an extension of Towle's recommendations for courses in social work education on human growth and behavior, and it includes normal behavior, abnormality and deviation, growth, maturation and change, and the helping process.[4] The level to which subject matter is applied is divided into the categories of individual, group, organization, community, and society. Each type of subject matter can be classified into each of five different levels. Hence, there are twenty categories (four types of subject matter times five levels) in which social research results can be organized. For example, the subject matter of growth, maturation, and change applied to the level of groups "might include the developmental processes and phases of families, friendship groups, problem solving groups, and therapy groups." [5] Although this scheme is potentially useful, it may be difficult to employ. It tends to emphasize subject matter related only to selected aspects of the social work curriculum, i.e., it too is not comprehensive. In addition, the categories are not mutually exclusive, which may lead to unreliability by different users of the system.

Maas devised a simpler and more comprehensive classification plan which has been used by social work scholars to "present critically what has been learned through systematic study, and may now be drawn upon for use in five fields of social service." This classification is not restricted to any discipline, and it includes: "research on (1) those persons or groups toward whom the field directs its services; (2) the social organization of agencies set up to give the services; (3) the social policies that orient the services; (4) the social work methods used with clients; and (5) the outcome of the services." [6]

This scheme has been employed successfully for reviewing knowledge from social research in family services, public welfare, child welfare, neighborhood centers and group work, and community organization and social planning. Furthermore, it is most useful for illustrating types of knowledge from social research that are pertinent to social work. For example, Briar reviewed research related to family services by locating studies with the following content areas: [7]

1. Related to Maas's first criterion, "those persons or groups toward whom the field directs its services," studies were reviewed on family organization and disorganization, the multi-

problem family, marital adjustment, the structure and dynamics of families, and characteristics of clients who receive social work services in family service agencies.

2. The content of research studies subsumed by the criterion of "the social organization of agencies set up to give the services" included knowledge on characteristic patterns of service such as how often clients are interviewed by social workers, knowledge about the uses of different recording systems, cost analyses of social work activities, staff turnover, worker satisfaction, and the process of supervision.

3. Research pertaining to the criterion of "the social policies that orient the services" consisted of knowledge related to the policies of the Aid for Dependent Children (AFDC) program— policies pertaining to whether AFDC mothers should work, whether day care centers should be established, and so forth.

4. Knowledge from social research relevant to the fourth criterion, "the social work methods used with clients," was organized under these categories: studies of reduced case loads, intensive casework, perceptions of social workers by their clients, the willingness of clients to be influenced by social workers, the attitudes of social workers toward the use of fees in casework practice, assumptions made by caseworkers in family service, and typologies of casework treatment.

5. Related to the criterion of "the outcome of the services," studies pertaining to the effectiveness and efficiency of social casework were presented—the relative efficacy of casework treatment as compared with no services, and the location of factors associated with successful treatments.

The types of knowledge illustrated above pertain to content areas relevant for social work. However, what is or is not "relevant" is subject to change, and a classification system that is useful today may be soon outmoded. There are currently changes taking place in the kinds of social problems that are regarded as important—changes in the helping professions with regard to priorities for service activities, changes in the characteristics and demands of client groups, changes in the allocations of monies for social agencies, and changes in society itself as a function of such social movements as Women's Liberation and Welfare Rights. All of these changes lead to variations in the functions and activities of social workers, which in turn lead to variations in the types of knowledge from social research that are pertinent to social work.

Levels of Knowledge

To increase the communications of research findings from social researchers to social workers, it is necessary that the same language be used in discussing knowledge—one that can be used for discussing knowledge within any content area. The classification of knowledge by levels is a language employed by social researchers to speak of the knowledge they attempt to secure by means of research strategies and observational techniques. Furthermore, the same classification can and should be used by social workers to understand and process the knowledge presented in the findings of social research. Levels of knowledge refers to a continuum which has increasing degrees of information value: concepts and variables, hypotheses, facts and empirical generalizations, and theory.[8]

CONCEPTS AND VARIABLES

Concepts are symbolic terms or labels for organizing experiences.[9] By providing a shorthand way of summarizing experiences, concepts can facilitate communication. Each profession or discipline has its own jargon or vocabulary which is comprised of a number of concepts. The concepts are the basic building blocks on which communication is based, for they describe succinctly those phenomena that relate to the interests, needs, activities, and expertise of the profession. Social workers use concepts such as movement, supportive treatment, social role, social functioning, group cohesiveness, reinforcement, power structure, bureaucracy, family stability, alienation, social adjustment, and inter-organizational linkages. Some of the concepts employed in social work are relatively unique to the profession, while others are incorporated from the social sciences, related professions, and society at large.

Although concepts have been defined and categorized in different ways by such methodologists as Zetterberg, Greenwood, and Goode and Hatt, there are two types of definitions that have been employed most often in social research and social work: the nominal definition and the operational definition.[10] A concept is nominally defined when it is defined in terms of other concepts, of which their meaning is assumed. One type of nominal definition is that of a dictionary definition, which follows the Aristotelian method of locating the concept within a general class and indicating the similarities and differences between the concept as a member of that class and other members of the class. For example, Ripple and Alexander devised a classification system for describing the types of problems that clients bring to social agencies, and they employed nominal definitions to distinguish between two types of conflict in the class of psychological problems:

> Psychological problems are described by four categories which are differentiated on the basis of whether or not there is a relatively defined focal aspect of the problem and what that aspect is. The first two, "interpersonal conflict" and "intrafamilial conflict," differ only in the number of persons involved in the conflict. Use of either category necessitates that there be overt conflict; this, however, does not necessarily mean violent quarreling, but rather that there is recognized differences and disagreement—between two people, if classified as interpersonal conflict; among three or more, if classified as intrafamilial conflict.[11]

A different kind of nominal definition is that of sensitizing through discussion of what the concept is intended to symbolize. This is especially useful for defining concepts which are relatively abstract and not easily definable by the Aristotelian procedure referred to above. Typically, the vehicle for nominal definitions of this type is the essay. An excerpt from Presthus' discussion on community power exemplifies this procedure:

> In this study, we shall conceptualize power as a system of social relationships. This presupposes in every community a certain ongo-

ing network of fairly stable subsystems, activated by social, economic, ethnic, religious, and friendship ties and claims. Such systems of interest, values, and power have desirable consequences for their members to the extent that they satisfy various human needs. In a sense, however, such subsystems are suprahuman, in that they tend to persist indefinitely and, more important, that their members may change but the underlying network of interrelated interests and power relations continues. The United States Senate provides an example of such an institutional system. It is a body with venerable customs, traditions, expectations, and rules that provide a given structure *within which* its members must learn to act. If they achieve and retain power as individuals, they do so within and through this larger social apparatus. Without the ability to form coalitions with like-minded colleagues, to avoid fracturing the prestige aspirations, seniority-based assignments and prerogatives, as well as the latent political commitments of their fellow members, no individual Senator can become powerful. In a word, his own power and effectiveness are inherently bound up in a social interpersonal system, with its own complex rules and expectations.

In community political life it seems that a similar conception of power may help us to give order and meaning to our mass of empirical data. We will look for discrete, yet overlapping, constellations of power, each with a major *raison d'être*, comprising individuals who share common social interests and attributes institutionalized in a given subsystem. We shall not, of course, find that such a subsystem is composed of homogeneous members fully committed to its norms, but rather that individuals have several overlapping group memberships, each of which tends to meet one or another of their varied interests—political, economic, ethnic, cultural, and so on. Simply put, individuals of similar interests combine to achieve their ends, and such combinations of the interlaced values and interests form subsystems of power. The community is composed of a congeries of such subsystems, now cooperating, now competing, now engaged, now moribund, in terms of the rise and fall of local issues. Some subsystems are more powerful than others; some more transitory; others persist, one supposes, because the interests which they institutionalize are persistent.[12]

A nominal definition helps to inform us of the intended meaning of a concept, however, it often leads to some ambiguity in communication because varying interpretations may be given to the words used to define the concept.

Another type of definition—the operational definition—specifies a concept more precisely in that it points to referents of the concept that can be observed directly or indirectly. An operational definition articulates those indices necessary for obtaining a measurement of the concept. In essence, it has the function of translating a concept into a variable, which is definable as a measurable dimension of a concept that takes on two or more values.[13] Thus, the variable referring to a person's age might be defined as the number of days the person has lived since birth, skill in typing might be defined operationally as the speed and accuracy with which one types dictated letters, and community participation might be defined as the number of community organizations to which one belongs.

The chief advantage of an operational definition is that it guides us to make similar observations, which can be communicated and repeated by independent investigators. Its primary disadvantage is that it is often an arbitrary definition, and it may bear little relation to the concept it is intended to represent. Yet, it is necessary that concepts be translated to variables through operational definitions if higher levels of knowledge, such as facts and empirical generalizations, are to be obtained.

HYPOTHESES: DESCRIPTIVE,
CORRELATIONAL, CAUSE-EFFECT

Hypotheses are statements of predicted relationships between two or more variables.[14] As statements of predicted relationships, they are neither true nor false. Their verification is based on empirical observations, which can be obtained by the strategies and observational techniques of social research.

There are three kinds of hypotheses: descriptive, correlational, and cause-effect.[15] These hypotheses form a continuum that is based on increasing amounts of information—with descriptive hypotheses containing the least and cause-effect hypotheses containing the most information.

Descriptive Hypotheses

Descriptive hypotheses are those hypotheses that state the existence of empirical regularities. They are usually concerned with the relative frequency of occurrence of some phenomenon, and they are often phrased in the form of questions such as the following: what is the number and proportion of dilapidated houses in a specified neighborhood? what are the incomes of males and of females who work in similar jobs? what proportion of persons who receive AFDC benefits are active in welfare rights organizations? what number and proportion of social workers who work for public agencies have participated in or are willing to participate in strikes to better their working conditions? what is the average length of time that social workers remain employed within one agency?

Essentially, descriptive hypotheses lead to information about frequency counts and proportions within one variable which is identified by another variable. For example, in the question, "what are the numbers and proportions of male and of female social workers engaged in private practice?" the social worker's gender is the variable within which frequency counts would be secured, while type of practice (private or not private) is the variable used for identifying which males and females should be counted.

As indicated by Goode and Hatt, some social researchers would not regard "descriptive hypotheses" as hypotheses because they lead to the accumulation of simple facts, which are of a low degree of abstraction and generality.[16] However, the compilation of simple facts is important for social work and, indeed, the objectives of many research studies are to provide such data. The verification of descriptive hypotheses leads to concrete information necessary for purposes of administration, social planning, and community organization.

Correlational Hypotheses

In addition to implying the existence of empirical regularities within variables, correlational hypotheses state the amount and / or the direction of the joint relationships between variables. These hypotheses are often in the form of declarative statements such as: there is a statistically significant correlation between anxiety and reading comprehension; there is a high inverse relationship between income and participation in community organizations, i.e., the higher the amount of income, the lower the degree of participation; there is a positive relationship between the I.Q. scores of clients and the number of interviews they have with caseworkers before termination of casework treatment, i.e., the higher the I.Q. scores, the higher the number of interviews completed; there is no relationship between unemployment and the incidence of marijuana smoking.

Correlational hypotheses lead to research investigations which aim to produce quantitative information pertaining to the joint distributions of the variables contained in the hypotheses. Thus, the results of research about correlational hypotheses are expressed in correlation coefficients or other statistical indices from which relationships among variables can be inferred. For example, there is a high, positive correlation ($r = +.80$) between income and the rate of juvenile delinquency; or there is a low, negative correlation ($r = -.10$) between the number of group meetings and the proportion of negative remarks made by group members; or a statistically significant proportion of high-income voters are more likely to vote for Republican candidates than for Democratic candidates (80 percent of a high-income group voted for Republican candidates, while 85 percent of a low-income group voted for Democratic candidates).

Some correlational hypotheses are stated less specifically than those above. Hypotheses regarding the location of variables associated with a specified variable may take the following form: what are the correlates of juvenile delinquency (a specified variable)—stability of family, number of previous offenses, age, grade point average in school, etc.? Thus, a question is asked which implies a series of correlational hypotheses: what is the relationship between stability of family and juvenile delinquency? between number of previous offenses and juvenile delinquency? between age and juvenile delinquency? and so forth.

Other correlational hypotheses are stated more precisely in that they involve the joint relationships of three or more variables. For example, there is a positive relationship between I.Q. scores and reading comprehension for persons with low degrees of anxiety, and a negative relationship between I.Q. scores and reading comprehension for persons with high degrees of anxiety.

Correlation does not imply causality. Thus, a correlational hypothesis about the relationship between low family income and the incidence of psychosis does not imply that low-income levels lead to psychosis or that psychotics are unable to work and consequently have lower incomes. Either of the variables, income level or psychosis, may lead to changes in the other, or both of them may be the result of still other variables.

Cause-Effect Hypotheses

While a correlational hypothesis states that a relationship exists between variables, a cause-effect hypothesis attempts to explain that relationship by specifying its cause. Cause-effect hypotheses state causality, and they also imply the existence of empirical uniformities within variables and the degree of joint relationship between variables. The simplest form of a cause-effect hypothesis includes two variables. One of these is the independent variable or presumed cause, and the other is the dependent variable or presumed effect. In the statement of a cause-effect hypothesis, it is posited that variable x, the independent variable, leads to changes in variable y, the dependent variable. For example, it might be hypothesized that mild aversion shock therapy with enuretic children will result in a reduction in bed-wetting—or stated in a different manner, those enuretics who receive mild aversion shock therapy are more likely to reduce their frequency of bed-wetting than those enuretics who do not receive mild aversion shock therapy.

Cause-effect hypotheses may be much more complex than a statement of relationship between two variables. For example, it may be posited that the joint occurrence of variables A and B (no employment and the presence of peers who are also unemployed) leads to variable C (increased thoughts about illegal activity), which in turn, coupled with the occurrence of D (increased opportunities for illegal activity), leads to E (a greater incidence of crime). However, cause-effect hypotheses employed in social research are typically stated in a simpler form, with only two or three variables included.

FACTS AND EMPIRICAL GENERALIZATIONS

The verification of hypotheses results in facts or empirical generalizations. Facts summarize quantitative information about descriptive hypotheses which are specific to the populations which are observed and are non-generalizable to other populations.* For example, the proportion of clients who are female in a particular family service agency might be observed as 45 percent, a figure which is not necessarily generalizable to other family service agencies.

Another example of a fact is the number of persons enumerated in a national census as of a specific date. Empirical generalizations are abstracted from facts. Thus, an empirical generalization resulting from observations about the proportions of males and females who are social workers might be that "With the exception of corrections, probation and parole, there are more females than males who work as social caseworkers in social agencies."

Empirical generalizations are also definable as verified correlational and verified cause-effect hypotheses. Hypotheses cannot be proved to be true for all time, everywhere, and under all conditions; however, evidence can be provided, from a series of replicated research studies, which can lead us to be relatively certain about the confirmation of hypotheses. To verify correlational hypotheses, evidence is required about the accuracy of measurement, the existence of the specified relationship among variables by statistical indices, and the generality of that relationship. More evidence is required for cause-effect hypotheses. As previously indicated in chapter one, the following types of evidence must be provided: 1) the specification of an accurate and generalizable

* Facts are defined narrowly to avoid the confusion which often results in attempting to differentiate them from empirical generalizations. Although it is possible for facts to be distinguished from empirical generalizations with respect to their relative differences in abstraction and generality, the distinctions are difficult to maintain. Indeed, facts may be regarded as low level empirical generalizations, while empirical generalizations may be conceived as high level facts!

relationship between the independent and dependent variables; 2) observations which indicate that the independent variable precedes the dependent variable in time; and 3) observations verifying that no variables other than the independent variable are responsible for the observed changes in the dependent variable.

There are more empirical generalizations abstracted from verified descriptive hypotheses than there are from verified correlational and verified cause-effect hypotheses. In other words, there are a greater number of available empirical generalizations at lower levels of knowledge. Nevertheless, there are many empirical generalizations related to all three types of hypotheses, and they have been reported by scholars who have reviewed social research studies. The following examples are illustrative:

Empirical Generalizations, Descriptive Hypotheses
1. "The child coming into foster home care comes, for the most part, from chronically deprived lower-class families facing crisis situations." [17]
2. "In every known human society, there is a prohibition against incest—i.e., against sexual relations or marriage with any member of the nuclear family and with some members of the extended family." [18]
3. ". . . control Ss who do not receive psychotherapy change positively as a group with the passage of time." [19]

Empirical Generalizations, Correlational Hypotheses
1. "Therapeutic progress varies as a function of therapist characteristics such as warmth, empathy, adequacy of adjustment, and experience." [20]
2. "The larger, the more complex, and the more heterogeneous the society, the greater the number of organizations and associations that exist within it." [21]
3. "The degree of congruence between the worker and the client in their definitions of the client's situation has been found to be strongly associated with continuance in all studies that have examined this factor." [22]

Empirical Generalizations, Cause-Effect Hypotheses

1. "Psychotherapy may cause people to become better or worse adjusted than comparable people who do not receive such treatment." [23]

2. "When a response is followed by punishment, the frequency or probability of recurrence decreases—where punishment is any event that runs counter to the existing set of motives, e.g., pain. Again, when punishment is withdrawn, the rate tends to recover." [24]

3. "When caught in cross-pressures between the norms of different groups of which he simultaneously is a member, the individual will suffer some emotional strain and will move to reduce or eliminate it by resolving the conflict in the direction of the strongest felt of his group ties." [25]

THEORY

The highest level of knowledge is theory. The major functions of theory are to describe and explain the interrelations of empirical generalizations and to provide conceptual systems from which hypotheses can be derived for empirical validation. A theory is not tested directly: hypotheses are deduced, and their verification or refutation contributes to the expansion or revision of the theory. There are no grand theories which interrelate empirical generalizations about psychological, sociological, economic, and other phenomena pertinent to social work. However, there are theories on a smaller scale which are useful as sources of hypotheses and possible explanations of social behavior. Thus, there are theories of learning, theories of personality development, theories of bureaucratic organization, theories of child development, theories of psychotherapy, theories regarding juvenile delinquency, theories of decision-making, and so forth.

The development of theory is a creative act, and it is not subject to codification. According to Greenwood, a theoretician identifies underlying themes that occur in a series of empirical generalizations, and he unifies the various themes into a single conceptual system.[26] For example, Hull developed a theoretical system for explaining empirical generalizations derived from experiments on learning by employing such theoretical constructs as reinforcement, generalization, motivation, habit strength, inhibition, oscillation, and response evocation. He described the process of theory construction as follows:

> Empirical observation, supplemented by shrewd conjecture, is the main source of the primary principles or postulates of a science. Such formulations, when taken in various combinations together with relevant antecedent conditions, yield inferences or theorems, of which some may agree with the empirical outcome of the conditions in question, and some may not. Primary propositions yielding logical deductions which consistently agree with the observed outcome are retained, whereas those which disagree are rejected or modified. As the sifting of this trial-and-error process continues, there gradually emerges a series of primary principles whose joint implications are more likely to agree with relevant observations. Deductions made from these surviving postulates, while never absolutely certain, do at length become highly trustworthy.[27]

Knowledge Objectives
of Social Research

In communicating their research results, researchers should indicate the levels of knowledge they sought, and they should report on the extent to which they are confident in having achieved those levels. Correspondingly, social workers should appraise research results and decide how confident *they are* of the researcher's achievement of knowledge. It is instructive, therefore, to summarize the objectives of research in terms of levels of knowledge, and then to specify criteria that can be employed to make confidence judgments about the attainment of those knowledge levels.

Social research has five knowledge objectives. They are the development of concepts, the formulation of hypotheses, the verification of descriptive hypotheses, the verification of correlational hypotheses, and the verification of cause-effect hypotheses. Although the formulation and verification of theory is an implicit goal of many social research studies, it is not included as a knowledge objective of social research for the following reasons: 1) There are no explicit procedures for developing theory through social research strategies and techniques; 2) The development of concepts and the formulation of hypotheses are related to theory development; 3) The verification of hypotheses is pertinent to the "testing" of theory; and 4) Theories about social work are not highly developed in terms of interrelating empirical generalizations.

The objective of developing concepts includes the specification and respecification of concepts for succinctly describing observational data, the refining of concepts so they can be converted to variables, and the development of procedures for the measurement of variables. A research study may include only one aspect of developing concepts, e.g., developing a scale to measure social adjustment; or it may include several aspects such as locating concepts, articulating nominal and operational definitions, and developing instruments for quantifying observations.

The formulation of hypotheses includes the articulation of descriptive hypotheses, correlational hypotheses, and / or cause-effect hypotheses. These hypotheses may be developed by such means as codifying qualitative impressions and processing quantitative data in secondary analyses. Research studies which seek to formulate hypotheses may also develop the variables basic to those hypotheses. Thus, they might have such combined objectives as formulating correlational hypotheses and operationally defining concepts.

Another objective is that of verifying descriptive hypotheses in order to produce simple facts and empirical generalizations. In this regard, research studies aim to produce such data as the demographic characteristics, opinions, and social, educational, and health needs of specific populations. The public opinion polls, community censuses, and epidemiologic surveys of the incidence and prevalence of disease are prototypes of research studies which seek to verify descriptive hypotheses.

Verifying correlational hypotheses is still another objective of social research. Many research studies, particularly surveys, have this objective in conjunction with that of verifying descriptive hypotheses, since data pertaining to both kinds of hypotheses can be gathered simultaneously. For example, there are research studies which have sought to verify both types of hypotheses by securing information about the utilization of health services by the poor and the relationship of knowledge of those services, and other factors, to utilization.[28]

The final objective with respect to knowledge-seeking activities of social research is the verification of cause-effect hypotheses, primarily by means of experimentation and the explanatory survey. Exemplary studies which attempt to verify cause-effect hypotheses are those which are concerned with evaluating the effectiveness of social work interventions. In this respect, two notable research studies are *Girls at Vocational High* by Meyer, Borgatta, and Jones and *Brief and Extended Casework* by Reid and Shyne.[29] Meyer et al. sought to test hypotheses regarding the efficacy of casework treatment with adolescent girls, while Reid and Shyne obtained data related to hypotheses about the relative efficacy of brief as compared to extended casework for families.

Criteria for Evaluating Levels
of Knowledge

Five criteria can be employed to evaluate the extent to which the knowledge objectives of social research have been achieved: concept translatability, hypothesis researchability, measurement accuracy, empirical generality, and internal control.[30] Combinations of these criteria are employed to evaluate evidence that is necessary for attaining various levels of knowledge. The criterion of concept translatability is used for evaluating the knowledge level of "developing concepts"; concept translatability and hypothesis researchability, for the "formulation of hypotheses"; concept translatability, hypothesis researchability, and measurement accuracy, for "the verification of descriptive hypotheses"; concept translatability, hypothesis researchability, measurement accuracy, and empirical generality, for "the verification of correlational hypotheses"; and all five criteria are applied for evaluating "the verification of cause-effect hypotheses."

CONCEPT TRANSLATABILITY

Concept translatability refers to the extent to which concepts are specified so that they can be transformed into measurable variables. Included in this dimension are the subcriteria of conceptual clarity, conceptual generality, sensitization, variable transformation, and index construction.

Concepts are conceptually clear if their nominal definitions are noncircular and unambiguous so that they lead to consistent interpretations. For example, the statement "intelligence is creativity" is not conceptually clear. It may be circular in that both concepts may symbolize the same phenomenon, which is essentially a "nondefinition" since no new information is provided. The statement may be intended to represent only one facet of intelligence, but that would be ambiguous unless it were followed up by qualifying information that differentiates other aspects of intelligence from the creative one.

Conceptual generality is a subcriterion that pertains to the extent to which concepts can be generalized for use in situations beyond the contexts of research in which they were generated. The greater the generality of the concept, the greater is its potential applicability and importance. The concepts of "learning," "stress," and "social class" are generalizable in that they can be used for viewing phenomena in a wide variety of cultural settings. Concepts are potentially more generalizable if they relate to, but can be differentiated from, other concepts employed for describing similar phenomena, e.g., the concept of interpersonal conflict as distinguished from intrafamilial conflict.[31]

Related to conceptual generality is the notion of "sensitization." Since many researchers claim that the value of concepts developed from social research is that of sensitizing us to become aware of important social phenomena,[32] it is necessary to appraise concepts by their sensitization values. A concept would have high sensitization value if it provided a different way of looking at social phenomena which influence subsequent practice, theory, or research. For example, the concept of subcultural differentiation which signifies that different groups may have discrepant customs, attitudes, and values has helped social workers make more realistic assessments of their clients' problems. Rather than assuming that the client's behavior is individually determined, social workers make diagnoses of individual behavior in the context of the client's subcultural milieu, whether it be comprised of Italian-speaking immigrants, middle-class Chicanos, or low-income Appalachian whites. A concept would have low sensitization value if it is merely another label for a phenomenon to which we are already sensitized. For example, nothing is added to the knowledge of a community organizer if the concept of "system disillusionment," conceived as equivalent to "anomie," is added to his conceptual system which already includes the concept of "anomie."

Variable transformation is a basic criterion for all quantitative research investigations. It refers to the identification of empirical referents which can be used in the operationalizations of concepts as variables. For example, the concept of social class can be transformed to a variable by the use of indicators such as amount of education, amount of income, and ranked prestige of occupation.[33] If a concept cannot be defined in terms of empirical referents, it cannot be measured. Although nonmeasurable concepts may have high sensitization values, such as the Freudian notions of super-ego and id, they are useless for empirical research which seeks to verify the relationship of those concepts to other concepts.

Index construction involves the linking of an operational definition of a variable to specific observational techniques. Identifying observable indicators of a concept is insufficient for purposes of measurement. One must also indicate how the observations are to be made and classified so that they comprise one of the scales of measurement—nominal, ordinal, interval, or ratio. For example, the variable of education may refer to different amounts of completed education, or its equivalent, in public schools in the United States. The completion of college might be regarded as a high amount of education, whereas an eighth-grade education or less might be conceived as a low amount of education. The data may be obtained from interviews and school records, and they could be classified into a nominal scale with mutually exclusive and exhaustive categories.

If, in the evaluation of a concept, all of the aforementioned criteria have been met; one would be highly confident in asserting that the concept has been sufficiently developed. It might be utilized for practice purposes, or it might be used in the development of higher levels of knowledge.

HYPOTHESIS RESEARCHABILITY

Hypothesis researchability is the extent to which an hypothesis is amenable to empirical verification through research strategies and observational techniques. It refers to the potential usability of formulated hypotheses. Included in the dimension of hypothesis researchability are these interrelated subcriteria: clarity of the hypothesized relationship between concepts, concept translatability for those concepts basic to the hypothesis, variable independence, hypothesis specificity, and feasibility.[34]

To evaluate the clarity of the hypothesized relationship between concepts, one should determine the type of hypothesis that is formulated, i.e., cause-effect, descriptive, or correlational. A cause-effect hypothesis is clear when the independent and dependent variables are delineated; and a descriptive hypothesis, when the basic variables for purposes of quantitative description are identified. Three steps can be taken to evaluate the clarity of a correlational hypothesis, e.g., an hypothesis regarding the relationship between the use of birth control methods (A) and anxiety about sex (B). First, one should be able to determine that it is not a cause-effect hypothesis, i.e., A does not cause B, nor do changes in B lead to changes in A. Second, one can determine whether the direction of the relationship between A and B is clear by observing whether statements such as the following are made: As the use of birth control methods *increases,* anxiety *decreases;* As anxiety *increases,* the use of birth control methods increases. Third, one can determine whether the amount of relationship between the variables is indicated by locating such statements as: There is *no statistically significant* correlation between anxiety and the use of birth control methods; or There is a *high degree of association* between the use of birth control methods and anxiety.

Another subcriterion is the concept translatability of the basic concepts in the hypothesis. One would apply the evaluative criterion of concept translatability, as previously discussed, to each variable in the above hypothesis, i.e., to anxiety and to the use of birth control methods. Both variables would be evaluated with respect to their potential for measurement.

Variable independence is still another subcriterion which relates to the researchability of hypotheses. Variables defined differently are independent, while variables defined in the same way are nonindependent. In an hypothesis that states a relationship between social class and poverty, the variables of social class and poverty may not be independent. Both variables may be operationalized in accordance with family income levels; and, by definition, a low-income family would also be designated as poor. Thus, the "hypothesis" is not researchable because the relationship between social class and poverty is predetermined—i.e., the variables are nonindependent.

Hypothesis specificity is a subcriterion used to evaluate an hypothesis in terms of the social context to which it is applicable. An hypothesis is specific when it includes statements about the population, time, and place to which it is pertinent. Two examples of relatively specific hypotheses are as follows: 1) There is no statistically significant relationship between anxiety and the use of birth control methods for low-income, female whites between the ages of 18 and 29 years who live in rural, mountainous regions of the United States; 2) There is a direct relationship between the use of birth control methods and anxiety for all women of child-bearing age in the early years of newly industrialized societies.

The subcriterion of feasibility refers to the extent to which hypotheses can actually be researched. In addition to the preceding subcriteria, feasibility refers to the following considerations:

1. *The hypothesized phenomenon should occur frequently enough so that observations can be made in planned research.* An hypothesis about the relationship between the use of birth

control devices and anxiety, in a particular country, is not re-searchable if the officials in that country forbid the use of birth control devices, and the citizens abide by that rule.

2. *The hypothesis should be one which allows for research within the ethical constraints of society and the professions.* It might be hypothesized that high-income persons are less likely than low-income persons to be influenced to use birth control methods by "brain washing techniques." This hypothesis is not (should not be) researchable if research for testing it involves the deliberate manipulation of "brain washing techniques," which is unethical.

3. *The indices constructed for measuring variables in the hypothesis should be suitable for recording observations.* Interviews may be the planned basis for obtaining information about the use of birth control devices among a particular subpopulation where medical records are not available. People in that subpopulation may not be willing to answer any interview questions, thus that observational technique would not be suitable.

MEASUREMENT ACCURACY

The verification of hypotheses depends on the quantification of data, which are evaluated in terms of their accuracy of measurement. There are four characteristics of quantitative data which relate to measurement accuracy: measurement classification, reliability, validity, and data processing.[35]

Measurement classification refers to whether or not data have been categorized by an appropriate measurement scale. A scale of measurement is appropriate if the data have the necessary properties for that measurement scale: mutually exclusive and exhaustive categories for a nominal scale; the properties of a nominal scale and order among the categories for an ordinal scale; the properties of an ordinal scale and equal distances between adjacent categories for an interval scale; and the properties of an interval scale and an absolute zero point for a ratio scale. Thus, data which meet the requirements of an ordinal scale could be classified appropriately in terms of an ordinal or a nominal scale, but not as an interval or ratio scale. When an inappropriate classification is made, a higher level of measurement is imputed to the data than is justifiable, and this leads to inaccurate conclusions.

The dependability of a measurement scale is evaluated by means of its reliability, i.e., interjudge agreement, test-retest reliability, and item equivalence. If the data are unreliable, one cannot be confident in the accuracy of measurement. For example, it might be reported that 20 percent of a population is psychotic. However, the figure of 20 percent is misleading if it turns out that the scale for classifying people into the categories of psychosis and several other psychiatric diagnoses is unreliable, e.g., there may be only 25 percent agreement among experienced psychiatrists who use the scale. To be regarded as adequately reliable, there should be approximately 70 to 80 percent agreement.[36]

Of fundamental importance in evaluating the accuracy of measurement is the validity of the data. The results of an investigation are not valid when the measurements do not correspond with the concepts in the hypotheses being tested. For example, a research study may be devised to report the prevalence of heroin usage among high school students. The variable of heroin usage may be defined in terms of the self-reports of high school students on questionnaires. The resulting information may be inaccurate—the students may lie about their use of heroin because they might be afraid that the disclosure of such information would be disadvantageous for them. If the responses to the questionnaires can be shown to be highly correlated with an independent measure of heroin usage (such as one which detects the presence of heroin in urine), their validity would be enhanced, and one would be more confident in the resulting statistics.

Validity should be evaluated with respect to the empirical evidence that is presented by researchers. When no evidence is available, one should appraise the contents of data-gathering instruments in terms of their relations to those concepts which are supposed to be measured. Further, one should evaluate the items of the instruments in light of their possible ambiguity. For example, results of public opinion polls may be inaccurate because the questions are misleading and equivocal for the respondents. Indeed, some respondents may not even understand the vocabulary used in the questions although they may answer them anyway!

A final characteristic is that of data-processing—the compilation and tabulation of data so that they can be analyzed by statistical means, and the accurate computation of statistical indices. An arithmetic error in calculation could lead to the reporting of inaccurate measurement even though the measurement scale is appropriate, reliable, and valid. In general, responsible researchers provide procedures for checking the tabulation of data, and their statistical computations are usually correct. Nevertheless, one's confidence in the accuracy of measurement is increased if he knows that researchers have employed systematic procedures for checking the internal consistency and accuracy of their computations.[37]

EMPIRICAL GENERALITY

Empirical generality refers to the extent to which there is evidence for generalizing the results of hypothesis-verification studies.[38] In particular, the verification of correlational and cause-effect hypotheses requires evidence related to empirical generality. There are two main sources of evidence that should be evaluated. One is representative sampling, the other is consistency of findings in replicated studies.

Representative sampling involves the use of systematic sampling procedures to provide research samples that have characteristics similar to the population to which the results would be generalized. Sampling procedures based on probability principles, such as simple random sampling, are the most reliable means of obtaining representative samples.[39] Thus, one may be reasonably confident in making generalizations to a larger population if the research sample has been drawn from that population on the basis of random sampling.

In many research studies it is not practically possible to employ random sampling techniques, and research samples may be selected by nonprobability methods. To evaluate the representativeness of such samples, one should specify the important defining characteristics of the population, and determine whether the sample is similar or different with respect to those characteristics. A study devised to verify a correlational hypothesis regarding voting preferences in national elections may be based on a sample of 1,000 low-income, minority group members. The results of that study would not be generalizable to all eligible voters because the sample is not representative of such important population characteristics as income, education, and possibly political party affiliation.

When research studies are repeated and the results are consistent, confidence in empirical generality is high. Correspondingly, confidence in empirical generality is low if replicated studies with different segments of the population do not lead to consistent results.

Three subcriteria can be used to evaluate the consistency of results in a number of replicated studies pertaining to a correlational hypothesis: 1) the correlations should be of approximately the same magnitude; 2) the correlations should be of the same direction, i.e., either positive or negative relationships; 3) the correlations should provide similar levels of statistical significance.

The consistency of results resulting from studies attempting to verify a cause-effect hypothesis can be evaluated by employing these criteria: 1) changes produced in the dependent variable should be of the same magnitude and direction; 2) changes observed in the dependent variable should occur consistently after the introduction of the independent variable; 3) changes observed in the dependent variable should consistently not be due to variables other than the independent variable.

Although there is no precise rule for determining what the correct proportion of similar results should be to achieve consistent findings, one could use the same criterion as employed for assessing percentage agreement: 70 to 80 percent of similar findings would be regarded as adequately consistent, while 85 percent and above would be regarded as highly consistent. Thus, if nine out of ten replicated studies produce similar results, one would be relatively confident of the empirical generality of those findings.

INTERNAL CONTROL

Internal control refers to the degree to which alternative hypotheses are eliminated as possible explanations of the changes observed in dependent variables.[40] As the number of alternative explanations decreases, the degree of internal control increases. There are five basic questions which can be raised for the purpose of determining how confident one is in the degree of internal control: 1) Is there evidence that the independent variable precedes the dependent variable in time? 2) Is there evidence that the changes in the dependent variable are not a result of normal growth and change in the research subjects? 3) Is there evidence that changes in the dependent variable are not a result of external events beyond the control of the researcher? 4) Is there evidence that changes in the dependent variable are not a result of contamination due to the biases of the researcher or of the research subjects? 5) Is there evidence that changes in the dependent variable are traceable to changes in the independent variable, rather than to the influence of antecedent or intervening variables? [41]

To increase confidence in the extent to which internal control has been achieved, two steps can be taken. First, one should conceive of alternative hypotheses that need to be ruled out as possible explanations for changes in the dependent variable. In this regard, the preceding questions could serve as stimuli. Second, one should evaluate the extent to which the research has eliminated alternative hypotheses as possible explanations. This can be done by referring to the empirical data and by observing whether procedures were employed in the research strategy for purposes of minimizing alternative hypotheses—such as randomization and the use of control groups.[42]

Suppose a research study was focused on testing an hypothesis regarding the influence of community organizers (the independent variable) on getting poor persons to vote more often (the dependent variable). It might have been found that more people voted, and it might have been concluded that there is a causal relationship between the independent and dependent variables. An evaluator of this knowledge might raise the following alternative hypotheses: 1) The increase in voting occurred prior to the intervention of community organizers; 2) More people voted because there were more eligible persons who reached voting age; 3) More people voted because they were influenced to do so through the mass media; 4) More people voted because they believed they would receive bonuses from the researchers, such as special clothing and food allowances; and 5) The increase in voting was due to an increase in public transportation facilities, good weather conditions, and a smaller proportion of the population that has major medical problems.

Having formulated a set of alternative hypotheses, the evaluator would note whether evidence related to the elimination of these hypotheses is available. Hypothesis 1 could be eliminated by observing that the researchers employed the procedure of experimentally manipulating the independent variable prior to the elections in which voting patterns were to be observed; hypotheses 2 and 5, by the provision of data which show, for example, that there are no increases in the number or proportion of eligible persons who reached voting age; hypothesis 3, by data which indicate that there is no relationship between influence attempts of the mass media and voting patterns; hypothesis 4, by evidence which indicates that the researchers were unknown or regarded as noninfluential to both voters and nonvoters who participated in the research.

Confidence in Social Research Knowledge

Four steps are involved in determining the extent to which one is confident in social research knowledge.[43] First, the research objectives are specified in terms of knowledge levels. Second, criteria are selected for evaluating the achievement of those levels. Third, confidence judgments are made about the adequacy

of evidence required by the evaluation criteria. Fourth, a determination is made about those levels of knowledge which have
been achieved.

The specification of knowledge levels and the criteria for evaluating them have been discussed previously. Table 1 is intended to serve as a guide for selecting those criteria that should
be applied for evaluating the various knowledge levels. Each
row in the chart includes a different knowledge level, and each
column includes a different evaluation criterion. As noted on the
chart, "X" is indicated for each evaluation criterion that is appropriate for evaluating each knowledge level. If an objective of
verifying descriptive hypotheses has been specified, one refers

Table 1
Criteria for Evaluating Knowledge

Knowledge Levels	Evaluation Criteria				
	Concept translatability	Hypothesis researchability	Measurement accuracy	Empirical generality	Internal control
Develop concepts	X				
Formulate hypotheses	X	X			
Verify descriptive hypotheses	X	X	X		
Verify correlational hypotheses	X	X	X	X	
Verify cause-effect hypotheses	X	X	X	X	X

NOTE: For each knowledge level, an "X" is indicated for each evaluation criterion that is appropriate for evaluating that level. Thus, concept translatability is appropriate for evaluating the level of developing concepts; concept translatability
and hypothesis researchability for evaluating the level of formulating hypotheses;
etc.

to the row which has the label "verify descriptive hypotheses," and he selects those criteria which are indicated by X's: concept translatability, hypothesis researchability, and measurement accuracy.* When the objective is to verify a correlational hypothesis, all of the criteria except that of "internal control" would be selected.

Although absolute standards are not available for making confidence judgments, it is possible to devise a rating scale to indicate the degree of confidence that is perceived by either the producers or the potential users of knowledge. The rating scale proposed here consists of three categories: low, moderate, and high confidence. Low confidence would be a judgment which indicates that the research has not produced a sufficient amount of evidence to meet the requirements of the evaluation criterion; moderate confidence would indicate that there is some evidence related to the criterion, but more is required; and high confidence signifies that the evaluator believes that the evidence is adequate enough to say that the criterion has been satisfied.†

Suppose that one is evaluating the knowledge generated from research studies which sought to verify a particular cause-effect hypothesis. The evaluator would apply the five evaluation criteria, and he would rate the extent to which he is confident in the research evidence for each criterion. High confidence ratings might be made for the criteria of concept translatability and hypothesis researchability, because the independent and dependent variables of the hypothesis are clearly stated, there is independence between the variables in the hypothesis, the

---

* Although empirical generality is not indicated as a criterion, it may be employed when the intent of the research is to produce empirical generalizations rather than simple facts which are to be descriptive only of a particular population.

† These ratings have been used by students in my research classes at the University of Michigan School of Social Work for evaluating social research knowledge, and moderate degrees of inter-judge agreement have been obtained. Nevertheless, it is not argued that there is convincing empirical evidence related to the reliability of these confidence ratings. Rather, it is maintained that the first step in using knowledge depends on the level of knowledge that is achieved, and the formation of confidence judgments is one way to determine the consistency of agreement about the achievement of knowledge.

hypothesis is specific, indices for measuring the variables are available, and the feasibility for carrying out the research is evident. With respect to the criterion of measurement accuracy, the researchers might have produced evidence which indicates that the variables are classified by the appropriate measurement scale, and that an acceptable degree of reliability has been achieved.

However, it might be observed that there is no evidence regarding the achievement or lack of achievement for predictive validity, although the contents of the measuring instruments appear to relate to the concepts measured. Therefore, the evaluator would rate his degree of confidence for measurement accuracy as moderate. It might be determined that the research findings are inconsistent from study to study, and that systematic sampling procedures were not used. This would lead the evaluator to rate his confidence in empirical generality as low. Finally, he might rate his confidence in internal control as low for the following reasons: control groups were not employed in any of the research studies, the possible effects of the researchers' biases were not controlled, there were other variables than the independent variable which were related to the dependent variable, and it was not demonstrated that the relationship between the independent and dependent variables persisted when those other variables were controlled.

To be confident in the level of knowledge being evaluated, the evaluator should rate his confidence as either moderate or high for all of the appropriate criteria. In the example above, the objective of verifying a cause-effect hypothesis has not been attained. However, one should not discontinue his evaluation efforts at that point. The evaluator could move down one level of knowledge and determine whether the criteria for verifying a correlational hypothesis have been met. Since the evaluator rated his degree of confidence in empirical generality as low, he would not be confident in asserting that a correlational hypothesis has been verified. The evaluator would be reasonably confident, however, in indicating that concepts have been developed, an hypothesis has been formulated for research, and a descriptive hypothesis has been verified. For example, the cause-effect hypothesis might have been concerned with the effects of group work treatment on attitude changes in parents of youngsters having difficulty in school. Although there might be insufficient evidence for indicating that there is a cause-effect or correlational relationship between group work and attitude change, there are simple facts which might be available, such as the distributions of parental attitudes toward the schools and the extent to which those attitudes change.

Sometimes one might determine that there are higher levels of knowledge than a researcher aimed to achieve. For example, a case study might have had as its purpose the development of concepts and the formulation of hypotheses. In the course of the study, quantitative data may have been gathered in relation to selected variables of interest. An evaluator may conclude that the evidence for measurement accuracy is high and that the data are sufficient for the verification of descriptive hypotheses specific to the context in which the research took place. Thus, Table 1 can be employed to select criteria for making confidence judgments about the specific knowledge objectives of research and about knowledge levels that are lower or higher than those research objectives.

Chapter 3

.^.

Using the Results
of Social Research

Two broad classes of knowledge from social re-
search can be used by social workers.[1] One is substantive knowledge, i.e., the results (or the findings) of social research investigations; the other is methodological knowledge, i.e., strategies
and observational techniques for information processing. Substantive knowledge is presented in concepts, hypotheses, facts,
and empirical generalizations. The dimensions involved in using
that knowledge are the subject of this chapter. Uses of methodological knowledge are discussed in chapter 4.

There is very little systematic research about how social work
practitioners use the results of social research. However, social
work educators have presented criteria for selecting knowledge
according to its soundness, relevance, and accessibility;[2] and
there is a body of empirical information regarding the utilization
process in the physical sciences, social sciences, agriculture, and

education.[3] From this work, principles can be derived for examining the extent to which a potential user (social worker) will *use* the results of social research. In this chapter, then, a conceptual scheme—integrating important notions from the literature in social work, the social sciences, education, and information science—is presented for the purpose of discussing those factors which may facilitate or impede the use of substantive knowledge from social research.

The Process of Using
Research Results

An example will illustrate the complexity of the process of using research results. Although hypothetical and somewhat idealized, it does suggest a range of activities involved in using research findings.

Miss Utilization (Miss U.) is a school social worker in a school district located in a small urban environment. She is responsible for providing social work services to one junior high school and four elementary schools. Miss U. consults with principals and teachers regarding children who have learning disabilities or are management problems in the classroom, and she provides counseling and referral services for those students, particularly for problems of home and school adjustment. Although Miss U. has a great deal of autonomy in her job, many of her tasks are dependent upon the school system in which she works. Hence, she maintains public relations and elicits cooperation from appropriate school personnel, and she solicits and screens referrals from teachers, guidance counselors, and principals.

One possible problem for which teachers may have sought Miss U.'s advice is classroom management. That is, disruptive and noisy students in class make it difficult for teachers to teach, and they may seek assistance in how to gain better control of their students. The social worker may have some advice in that regard. She may suggest that disruptive students should be removed from the classroom or, perhaps, that she should see the students on an individual basis to discern whether their difficulties are related to circumstances outside of the school setting. However, Miss U. may be uncomfortable about giving that advice. She may have employed such ideas in the past, but they did not seem to work in that the problem of disruptive students persisted.

Miss U. is more interested in "doing" than in reading literature that may pertain to active work with her cases. Yet, she occasionally reads the professional literature in social work, education, and the psychology of children. Because she is sensitive to the problem of classroom management, she may have read an article reporting some research results on the control of classroom behavior by using systems of positive reinforcement and token economy, i.e., principles involved in behavior modification. At first blush, she thought the authors proclaimed too much and that the techniques employed seemed to smack of "control" and "lack of freedom." But she read that the results indicated there was a greater degree of classroom control (the noise level was reduced), and an increase in teacher and pupil satisfaction. Moreover, increases in learning were reported. Miss U. might have thought, "The results are interesting, but I'll wait and see." So she put the study aside and did not consciously think of using the results of research in her practice.

Several months later, she attends a social work conference in New York City. She notes that there is a workshop on classroom management concerned with discussions and applications of the most recent research findings in that area. Miss U. decides to attend the workshop. To prepare for the workshop, the participants are asked to read several articles. After reading the articles, she begins to wonder how accurate the research knowledge is, so during the workshop she raises questions about confidence in knowledge. She asks questions about the empirical generality, measurement accuracy, and internal control of the research studies presented, and lively discussions ensue—which, to her, make for more interesting research presentations. The research results appeared to be consistent from school to school, and from classroom to classroom; behavior modification techniques were regarded as relatively effective for increasing cooperation between disruptive students and teachers. Although the evidence for internal control in each of the studies was not convincing, Miss U. and other participants are highly confident in asserting that the knowledge was at the level of a verified correlational hypothesis.

At the workshop Miss U. meets an old friend, a fellow student in a graduate school of social work. Her friend, Miss F., is also a school social worker and is employed in a school district in another state. Much to her surprise, Miss U. finds that her friend has used some of the techniques described in the workshop. Miss F. believes the techniques are potentially useful, but she thinks they are not too different from techniques that she learned in school. As a result of their discussion, it becomes clear to Miss U. that the knowledge is relevant in that it directly relates to the school social worker's job. Miss F. describes how students were given bonus points (which led to rewards) for completing work within class and for keeping the noise level down. After the students received a specified number of bonus points, they were allowed to exchange them for some preferred activity, such as extra recess time or visits to museums. Many more practical details of the positive reinforcement techniques of behavior modification are discussed. It becomes evident to Miss U. that the variable of positive reinforcement is accessible in the school setting, i.e., it can be controlled by manipulating the bonus points attached to completing certain classroom requirements. Furthermore, the hypothesis that the use of positive reinforcement techniques would lead to a reduction in the noise level is testable in the practice situation through classroom observation and self reports of teachers and students.

Miss U. is gradually influenced (by her own dissatisfaction of previous knowledge, by her readings and discussions at the workshop, and by her friend) to be receptive to the knowledge about positive reinforcement and classroom management. Some of the ideas of behavior modification, however, seem antithetical to the basic frame of reference within which she is operating as a social worker. She has predominantly an individualistic orientation to behavior based on notions of ego psychology, and she is aware of some discussion in the profession about behavior modification points of view as opposed to psychodynamic ones.

In essence, she is struggling with whether she should, could, or would change from one position to the other, or attempt to integrate the knowledge from both behavior modification and ego psychology. To change perspectives, she would have to learn a new set of principles and a new vocabulary, and this would require a major investment of time and energy. At this point, then, Miss U. could reject using the knowledge of research results in behavior modification techniques for disruptive students in classrooms. She may not be willing to devote the time to learn a new set of principles, or she may believe that she could not incorporate the knowledge if it does not coincide with her theoretical framework. However, she may subscribe seriously to the notion of accountability. If those "new" techniques appear to be more effective than her existing ones, she may be even more receptive to the knowledge in that she is willing to invest time in attempting to apply it.

Miss U. returns from the social work conference to her job, and she thinks a little more about the behavior modification techniques discussed at the workshop. She talks about it with some other social worker friends. One, Mr. H., regards himself as humanitarian, and he raises the issue of whether "control" is unethical. Is classroom management a form of social control which dehumanizes the students? Here, Miss U. must decide whether the knowledge is consonant with her system of values—i.e., whether the knowledge coincides with her preferences of desirable behavior for social workers, teachers, students, and so forth. If she decides that classroom management techniques are unethical, she will not apply the knowledge in her practice. Although she may not be too sure whether "control" is ethical, she may proceed to discuss the techniques with personnel at one of the schools where she works.

Miss U. discusses ideas of classroom management with an assistant principal, Mr. P., who is potentially interested, but is concerned about whether the school will be accused of trying to "buy off" the students with rewards. Mr. P. knows of a Dr. A. who has conducted practice and research in the area of classroom management, and Mr. P. suggests that Dr. A. might be willing to talk with them.

A conference is scheduled with Dr. A. In that meeting, the topics of ethics and control are discussed. Dr. A. asserts that control already exists in the school—students are suspended, removed from classrooms, given grades, etc. He points out that much of that control is exhibited in the form of punishment. Furthermore, Dr. A. says that rewards offered in classes need not be in terms of money; they could be desired classroom activities which may heighten, rather than diminish, the students' expressions of individuality within the classroom.

Having decided that the use of behavior modification techniques is ethical, Miss U. may be convinced that the knowledge should be applied in the schools were she works. But, the process of using the knowledge is more complex than that. Miss U. works in an organization, the school setting, and the knowledge must also be consonant with the values and priorities of the organization before it can be applied. Miss U. has already consulted with an important person in the organization, Mr. P.; other persons who might be involved are the superintendent of schools, principals, teachers, students and their parents, and representatives of the teachers' union. The social worker and Mr. P. may want to try out behavior modification techniques in those classrooms that have reputations for being unmanageable; but in order for the techniques to be used, there must be voluntary cooperation on the part of the teachers—if participation were mandatory, it might be resented, particularly if the teachers believe they are being singled out for "bad" performance.

The knowledge cannot be applied unless the organization has the capability to implement it. Will those in decision-making positions allow behavior modification techniques to be employed? Will resources be made available for using those techniques? What costs of time and manpower are necessary? A series of questions like these might be raised by key persons in the school system. After several discussions with such persons, it might be decided to implement the knowledge (or reject it). In this instance, a decision might be made to allow for the demonstration of behavior modification techniques on a trial basis. Permission may be granted to try out the techniques in several classrooms where teachers would volunteer as participants.

Dr. A. may be hired as a consultant, and he may work with Miss U. and several teachers in setting up the techniques for use in three classes. This may involve meetings in which the purposes of the techniques and the demonstration are clarified, and it may also entail a number of training sessions. The demonstration may be conducted in such a way that student and teacher reactions are elicited. Of utmost importance is the workability of the techniques. If the disruptive behaviors in classrooms diminish, other teachers may be more willing to use behavior modification techniques for classroom management and, consequently, Miss U. may be more certain about the advice she would give teachers trying to reduce disruptive behaviors among their students.

Communications of Substantive Knowledge

TRANSMITTING KNOWLEDGE

Knowledge must be clearly transmitted before decisions can be made about applying it. In the preceding chapter it was assumed, for purposes of presentation, that: 1) there is faithful transmission from researchers to social workers; 2) both senders (social researchers) and receivers (social workers) could employ the same criteria for making confidence judgments about the levels of knowledge achieved by social research. The latter assumption depends upon the effective transmission of research findings, which may or may not be realized. Social workers may not receive the "messages," or there may be *noise* within the communication system—i.e., what one receives may not be the same as the "knowledge message" which was sent. The knowledge could be distorted as it flows through various communication channels. For example, one person may read a research report and draw inappropriate conclusions about the substantive knowledge. In personal conversation, he may pass that knowledge on to another person who, in turn, may convey to others only those portions of the "knowledge" he can remember.

As implied by Menzel, it is desirable to take a systemic view of communications in order to devise principles for increasing the effectiveness of communicating research results.[4] The transmission and reception of messages is conceived as a set of interaction processes in a social system, which includes a number of transmission sources. Referring to the example of the process of using research results, it is readily seen that the reception and utilization of knowledge was dependent upon the social interactions in which Miss U. engaged. In particular, it can be noted that various sources of communication were used. Miss U. did not simply read a journal, and then apply that knowledge. She was receptive to the communications, and she received and attempted to digest knowledge from the literature, a workshop, friends, a consultant, the assistant principal—all sources of potential knowledge or of access to knowledge regarding the use of behavior modification techniques for classroom management. This illustrates an important principle of communications theory: "Several channels may act synergistically to bring about the effective transmission of a message." [5] In other words, repetition of a message from different communication sources is often necessary for effective transmission, and this principle implies that one source, such as a written research report, may be insufficient.

Sources of communication can be regarded as formal or informal. Formal communications are transmitted through the media (such as professional journals, newspapers, television, and films), training centers, professional conferences, and workshops. Informal communications are unplanned, person-to-person communications—through conversation, correspondence, group discussions, and so forth. Both sources of communication play important roles in the effective transmission of knowledge.[6] Informal communications bring messages to persons, groups, and organizations who might not otherwise have received them, while formal communications give the necessary information for making appropriate confidence judgments about the level of knowledge being communicated. Without informal communications, many social workers may not be aware of knowledge available through more formalized sources. If formal sources are not employed, the knowledge received may be distorted.

In addition to repetition through formal and informal sources, communications theory implies another important principle: the language of the knowledge transmitter should be compatible with that of the receiver.[7] There is no point in receiving communications which are unintelligible. In this regard, the notions about levels of knowledge discussed in chapter 2 were conceived as a device for enhancing language compatibility. That is, a common vocabulary was presented which relates to substantive knowledge, and which could be employed by both social researchers and social workers.

RECEIVING KNOWLEDGE

Although knowledge receptivity is discussed later in the chapter as a key criterion of the application of research findings, it is necessary at this point to consider three overlapping and interrelated dimensions which are preconditions for the reception of research communications by social workers: organizational relatedness, identification, and participation. All of these dimensions have to do with the attitudes and relationships of social workers (as potential receivers) to transmitters of social research results.

Organizational Relatedness

Most social workers are employed by social agencies, and they are affected by the administrative structures and operational priorities of those agencies. If the executive level of a social agency regards the use of research knowledge as important, it is likely to include research or knowledge utilization activities within its structure.[8] Organizational relatedness is determined by the extent to which a social agency is structurally related to research. A continuum of organizational relatedness consisting of five types of agencies would be one ranging from no research to a demonstration-practice program where the entire operation is related to research:

1. *Agencies with no research activity* are those in which research is given a low priority by both the administrative organization and practicing social workers.

2. *Agencies with some research activity* encourage staff members to engage in research efforts on a small scale. A few individuals may engage in projects (which may constitute less than 5 percent of their working time) such as the following: reviewing taped recorded interviews by content analyses; relating census-type information regarding client characteristics to judgments of success; locating gaps in service delivery by reviewing statistics for clients who "drop out" or do not participate in the service functions of social agencies.

3. *Agencies with contracted research* employ outside researchers for such purposes as evaluating the organizational effectiveness and efficiency of the agency, and for testing different service delivery systems. In these agencies, specific problems are located by administrators and / or practitioners, and researchers are hired to produce knowledge pertinent to solving those problems.

4. *Agencies with research departments* have formalized within their operational structures the establishment of research. Research departments may have the following functions: compiling agency statistics on what happens to clients who are processed by social agencies; evaluating social work efforts; developing knowledge pertinent to administration and direct practice.

5. *Agencies subsidized primarily by demonstration-research funds* are essentially demonstration programs which are set up on provisional bases. Research is built-in as an integral part of these programs. For example, a methadone program may be

established to rehabilitate heroin addicts by substituting methadone for heroin and by ultimately attempting to reduce methadone dosages. Job training, counseling, etc., may be included in this type of program which has the primary purpose of demonstrating its effectiveness in reducing drug addiction. Research is conducted to describe the program and to evaluate its successes and failures.

Obviously, the above types do not exhaust the possibilities of organizational relatedness. For example, some agencies may include a combination of research efforts—an agency may have a research department, encourage practitioners to engage in research, and hire outside researchers for special types of assistance. However, social agencies do vary in their degree of structured research activities, and the above types are suggestive of what is meant by increasing amounts of organizational relatedness. Agencies which have high degrees of organizational relatedness have direct linkages to research transmitters, and practitioners are physically close to the transmission sources.[9] Thus, social workers are more likely to receive research communications (particularly of research conducted in those agencies) when they work in agencies with high degrees of organizational relatedness than when they work in agencies with low degrees of organizational relatedness.

Identification

Identification, as used here, is the social workers' belief in the legitimacy and value of social research. Social workers who are closely identified with the goals of research are more likely to "tune in" and receive research communications than those social workers who do not value research.

To explicate further the dimension of identification, one can conceive a continuum of the relationship of research goals to practice goals. At one end of the continuum are those practitioners who do not regard social research as relevant to direct services. They would maintain that social research is for academicians and theoreticians, but not for direct practice because of the following reasons: research does not generate results which allow practitioners to make predictions about individuals; research information takes too much time to obtain; when research information is available, it is not in a form which is immediately useful, i.e., it is too abstract. At the other end of the continuum are those practitioners who over-identify with the goals of research. They may be in awe of research methodology, and believe that it always provides "scientific conclusions" about social phenomena. Some practitioners may even hold research knowledge above "practice wisdom." Because they believe that they have virtually no knowledge about the effectiveness of social work, they may expect research findings to provide guidelines for practice.

Between the two extremes, an under- or over-identification with research goals, there are those who regard social research (in social work) and social work as having a common goal: the improvement of social work practice. Practitioners provide questions which stimulate social research, and social research is a tool for developing and evaluating practice knowledge. Those social workers may be practitioner-researchers who spend their time equally in practicing social work and in conducting research related to practice, or they may use research skills as part of their practice—the administrator who initiates a monitoring system for evaluating his organization, the community organizer who develops profiles of community needs, the behavioral therapist who obtains measurements related to client change.

Social workers who do research in practice or who use research skills in their work are more likely to receive research communications than those social workers who do not identify with the goals of social research. Although social workers who over-identify with research are more likely to be receptive, they may distort research communications by presuming that the substantive knowledge is more accurate than it actually is.[10]

Participation

The dimension of participation overlaps with those of identification and organizational relatedness. It refers to the extent to which social workers are involved in the research prior to the communications of research findings. For example, social workers may have served as interviewers in a research project aimed at describing the attitudes of people who were eligible for, but did not utilize, available health and welfare services. The generalizations derived from the data may be particularly meaningful for those social workers, since they represent the results of work in which they were engaged. Hence, research results have a better chance of being communicated and being used if social workers participate and are involved in the research.[11]

In summary, then, knowledge can be transmitted through various media; and repetition in communication is likely to lead to reception of that knowledge—as long as the transmitters send messages through formal and informal channels which reach the audience of receivers. Knowledge that is produced within an organization can be transmitted to members of the organization quickly and efficiently because of physical proximity and structured linkages. Moreover, those practitioners who identify with research are more likely to receive knowledge messages than those who do not. And if social workers participate in some aspects of the research prior to the transmission of knowledge, they will probably be interested in and receptive to communications of the research results.

Criteria for Applying
Social Research Results

Six criteria are pertinent to transmitting, receiving, and using social research findings: confidence in knowledge, relevance, accessibility, receptivity, value-consonance, and capability for implementation. The criteria of confidence, relevance, and accessibility are pertinent to both the transmission and the reception of knowledge messages, while the other criteria are regarded as most important for the reception and utilization of those messages.

CONFIDENCE IN KNOWLEDGE

A table for selecting criteria for making confidence judgments was provided in chapter 2, and the reader should refer to it to review dimensions for appraising the results of social research. It is further recalled from the preceding chapter that to facilitate research communications two recommendations were made: 1) Social researchers should transmit research results with due consideration to the appropriate levels of knowledge that have been produced and to their degrees of confidence (low, moderate, high) in that knowledge; 2) Social work practitioners should have enough information about the research procedures so they can evaluate research knowledge and make their own determinations of confidence.

It is imperative that social researchers communicate appropriate levels of knowledge so that social workers are not influenced to make too much or too little out of research findings. On the other hand, it is important for social workers to make their own confidence judgments since they are the ones who will be dealing with the problems of applying that knowledge.

With respect to the transmission of research results, there is often a presumption by researchers and by publishers of research that there should be "statistically significant" results and / or *high degrees of association* (e.g., among the variables in correlational hypotheses) before the findings can be considered to be of value. In essence, there may be a predisposition to underreport zero-order relationships among variables. Within our perspective of levels of knowledge, it is clear that negative and zero-order findings should be reported, as well as positive findings. Indeed, this type of knowledge may represent much of what we have learned from social research. Again, referring to the principle of accountability, it is important to know whether models of practice are ineffective, or that theoretical biases are in error, or that certain procedures used in social work are unnecessary. Of course, one should evaluate the reporting of negative or zero-order relationships with the same caution that he would use in appraising positive findings. Was the research carefully conceived and executed, and are the results empirically generalizable and accurate?

An example of the reporting of a zero-order relationship is observable in Kadushin's review of findings in adoptions research.[12] He evaluated and summarized a number of research investigations which indicated that there is virtually no relationship between characteristics of adoptive parents and the subsequent (after adoption) adjustments of their adopted children. Yet, many social workers in adoption agencies have concentrated their efforts, over the years, in matching the characteristics of adoptive parents to those of adopted children, with the goal of fostering social adjustment. The implication is that the efforts of social workers should not be concentrated in the selection phase of adoption; the workers' time and energy might be spent better in dealing with the adjustment phase of adoption when the adoptive parents and children are living together.

RELEVANCE OF CONTENT

A social worker may be highly confident in the knowledge that is transmitted by social researchers, but he may not use that knowledge because he regards it as irrelevant. Of course, social research knowledge need not be pertinent to all aspects of social work, but it should be relevant to some. From the practicing social worker's point of view, the contents of knowledge messages are relevant when they pertain to his tasks and functions.[13] Obviously, what is currently relevant is influenced by the functions of agencies where social workers are employed and by the specific tasks they perform; ultimately, however, decisions regarding relevance are made by social workers within their own frames of reference. Knowledge that is regarded as important by community organizers may be deemed as having little value for social caseworkers; knowledge about group dynamics may be relevant to group workers, but irrelevant to policy developers. To illustrate "relevance" as it pertains to different subdisciplines within social work, examples are provided for each of three guidelines below:

1. *Contents of research knowledge are relevant when they*

relate to what is done currently or what could be done in the daily work of social workers.

Social caseworkers who work in family service agencies often engage in marital counseling. They may use therapeutic procedures such as behavior modification and conjoint family therapy. Substantive knowledge from social research is relevant when it pertains to the effectiveness and applicability of those techniques for the diagnosis and treatment of marital problems. Relevant knowledge for a group worker who works in a residential treatment center for emotionally disturbed children may include such topics as the effects of group living on individual treatment, and techniques for dealing with hyperaggressive children in groups. A community organizer who is attempting to organize a neighborhood may regard the following as relevant: the selection of appropriate strategies for organizing low-income residents, the location of key issues and problems, and economical ways to engage representative persons in the neighborhood for discussing and taking appropriate actions on neighborhood problems. The administrator and policy developer of a community mental health agency may be interested in the incidence and prevalence of mental disease, the extent to which services are available for mental health needs, and the utilization of services by potential clientele.

2. *Contents of research knowledge are relevant when they relate to an understanding of individual, group, organizational, or community attitudes and behaviors that may impinge on or facilitate social work activities.*

The social caseworker deals with a variety of other agencies in his contacts with clients. Knowledge of the ways in which those agencies function and are interrelated with respect to their potential as referral sources (e.g., legal, medical, psychiatric agencies) is important. Moreover, an understanding of subcultural influences may aid the caseworker in his diagnostic and treatment formulations. A group worker needs to have knowledge about organizations and community pressure groups. For example, he may find that group work in a school is affected by class schedules and other requirements for students within the organization of the school. Or, a community group living situation for drug addicts might be affected by "the neighbors" who do not want to have "those types of persons in the neighborhood"; and pressures are created to have the addicts moved. A community organizer may need to know about similar pressures that are created in a community with respect to an organization of minority group members. He may be concerned with locating sources of community power that might support such an organization; thus, knowledge about community leadership and of community influences would be relevant. An administrator also may be interested in sources of power as they influence financial allocations made to his agency, while the policy developer may benefit from knowledge that pertains to the effective and efficient delivery of social service systems.

3. *Contents of research knowledge are relevant when they relate to the social problems social workers deal with through their work with client groups and organizations.*

Social agencies may deal primarily with particular kinds of social problems—e.g., mental health agencies, with mental illness; probation agencies, with crime and delinquency; welfare rights organizations, with poverty and public welfare. Obviously, social workers regard knowledge as relevant when it is about social problems their agencies are concerned with. Social workers, however, often deal with a gamut of social problems which are not of primary concern to the agencies in which they work. For example, a social caseworker in a child guidance clinic may be attempting to foster a better relationship between a mother and her daughter. The mother may be a heroin addict, and this may affect the mother-daughter relationship. Thus, the caseworker may need to know something about the problem of heroin addiction and be able to locate other community sources for helping the mother if there are no resources in the caseworker's agency for such help.

An agency administrator needs to be attuned to increasing or decreasing emphases given to social problems in the community. For example, alcoholism and crime may be increasing among adolescents. An administrator of a family service agency may have no programs which deal with the problem. The agency may be responsive by changing its priorities and devising new treatment and referral programs. On the other hand, the priorities of the agency may not change in relation to the problem of adolescent crime and alcoholism. However, the priorities of funding sources, such as United Funds may change; and those funding sources allocate annual funds on the basis of whether or not social agencies have the same priorities that they do. Thus, administrators need to be aware of social problems and the priorities related to solving those problems by the community, their agencies, and their sources of financial support.

ACCESSIBILITY OF KNOWLEDGE

Accessibility of knowledge includes both its availability and its possible use in practice.[14] Knowledge that is made public and effectively communicated through information channels is available, however, available knowledge is not necessarily usable. To determine the potential usability of substantive knowledge from social research, social workers can employ four overlapping and interrelated dimensions: engineerability, strategic value, location value, and analogy.

Engineerability

Engineerability is the extent to which variables from research can be identified and manipulated in the practice situation, with the expectation that manipulation will lead to observable changes.[15] Thus, the dimension refers primarily to the knowledge level of facts and empirical generalizations, and it presumes that social workers can control phenomena that take place in practice. For example, there may be an empirical generalization which asserts that group members are more likely to attend group meetings when they are positively reinforced for their contributions to those meetings. If the group worker can specify what is meant by reinforcement and manipulate it in the practice situation, it is knowledge that is engineerable and, therefore, accessible.

Another example is that of an administrator who may be interested in obtaining increased amounts of productivity from his staff, i.e., more interviews, more group meetings, more low-income clients engaged in social work treatment, and so forth. A relevant empirical generalization may be made available to him: close supervision leads to lower productivity than does general supervision.[16] The administrator may attempt to control the rate of productivity by changing the supervisory structure in his agency from close to general supervision. If close supervision is operationalized by such indicators as large amounts of time in supervisory conferences and supervisory review of all decisions made by supervisees, then the structure of supervision can be potentially controlled by requiring, for example, that less time be spent in supervisory conferences. Of course, the supervisors *themselves* must make changes in the ways in which they supervise and, although knowledge regarding supervision is accessible, it may not be implemented because of the supervisors' unwillingness to do so. Nevertheless, the essential point here is that knowledge is accessible when the variables from research can be operationally defined and controlled in the practice setting.

Strategic Value

Strategic value is the extent to which research knowledge can lead to hypotheses and / or strategies in social work practice. The research knowledge may be either at the levels of hypotheses or of facts and empirical generalizations. For example, it may be shown that there is a high correlation between deteriorated housing conditions and tuberculosis. Although the knowledge may not be sufficient to indicate that tuberculosis is caused by deteriorated housing conditions, one might hypothesize that changes in housing—i.e., repairs, suitable garbage facilities, heating, etc.—will result in lower rates of tuberculosis. This may lead to efforts for making changes in housing policies and to implementing those policies by standardized guidelines and enforcement procedures. This knowledge is accessible in that some degree of control can be obtained over the key variables and, although one is not certain that the desired result will occur, it can be tested in the practice situation.

Strategic value, or suggestions for procedures that can be introduced in practice, may also be derived from research studies which formulate hypotheses. For example, an hypothesis may be developed from a study concerned with the ways in which psychotherapists deal with aggression in clients. It might be asserted that when aggressive behavior is dealt with directly in psychotherapeutic interviews clients are more likely to respond to direct suggestions made by therapists. Psychotherapists, perhaps caseworkers who have usually ignored aggressive comments made by clients, may try out the idea in practice. Another example is that of an hypothesis which may be derived from a study of the experiences of community organizers in organizing public welfare recipients. The hypothesis might state that organizational attempts are more successful (in terms of numbers of persons involved, continued participation, and decisions made in public welfare offices) when the targets of organization work on an issue that has immediate import for them. This knowledge is accessible in the form of a strategy for practice. The community organizers seek expressed interests from the people they wish to organize, and they attempt to locate issues of concern in the area where the people live. *If* they locate common issues that have immediate import (e.g., clothing allowances in winter months), then they can observe in practice what effect this strategy has on their organizational efforts.

Location Value

Much of the knowledge produced from social research is at the level of concepts. This kind of knowledge is accessible when it has location value, the extent to which the concepts can assist the social worker in locating problems and / or solutions for problems in his practice. For example, a group worker may observe that his group of "headstart mothers" (low-income mothers of children enrolled in a federally sponsored pre-school program) is inattentive in group sessions. Employing the concept of anomie (i.e., alienation from institutions and perceived lack of influence on those institutions), he may attempt to observe whether or not the group members are apathetic because they believe they have no choices or no influence on their children's education. The group worker may start discussions in accordance with this perspective by asking group members about their perceived degrees of influence; and if they feel powerless, he might try to motivate them to discuss what they could do about it. Therefore, the concept leads to the articulation of questions related to practice, and it may serve to locate possible problems that the group worker and his group need to handle. Although this kind of knowledge is important for providing perspectives for viewing practice, it is less precise than knowledge from empirical generalizations in that it does not offer prescriptions—i.e., direct guidelines for what to do in one's work.

Analogy

Many social research studies focus on phenomena that do not appear to be pertinent to social work practice. However, the results of those studies may be accessible by analogy—the process of making inferences "that certain admitted resemblances imply further probable similarity." [17] For example, substantive knowledge may be accumulated about the effects of sensory deprivation on a variety of animal species; and, for the sake of presentation, let us assume there is little knowledge about the effects of sensory deprivation on humans. Although the process of extrapolating knowledge from lower to higher order species may not produce accurate generalizations, it may lead to hypotheses which a social worker can try in his practice. One hypothesis may be that sensory deprivation (i.e., lack of external stimuli in one's environment) is detrimental to one's mental health. A hospital administrator may regard the isolation of patients as analogous to the isolation of animals in cages. This might compel him to consider whether different types of hospital environments might be more stimulating to hospital patients. Hence, he might plan for brightly colored rooms, patient access to recreational-type facilities, and opportunities for social interactions with other patients and the hospital staff.

That the use of analogy demands an active imagination is further illustrated in the following example. It might have been demonstrated in a series of experiments with humans that feedback of performance enhances a group's productivity in miniscule tasks such as solving crossword puzzles. Certainly, the task is not the same as that of a group of parents trying to come up with ways to deal with problems like the reactions of other children to their mentally retarded offsprings. However, one might use this knowledge by abstracting the concepts from the research (feedback, group productivity), making analogies to tasks more pertinent to social work, and trying out the resulting hypotheses. Thus, the group worker may start with a relatively simple task for his group, such as writing one positive and one negative statement about mentally retarded children. A task would be selected that could be easily completed. This provides a context in which the group worker can give "feedback" to the group. Subsequently, increasingly difficult tasks would be performed, with the group worker continuing to provide feedback. Eventually, the group members may be able to deal with the more complex task of providing constructive suggestions for increasing positive reactions in others about their mentally retarded children.[18]

KNOWLEDGE RECEPTIVITY

It was indicated previously that the reception of knowledge depends to a considerable extent on organizational relatedness, identification, and participation—conditions which facilitate the delivery of knowledge messages from transmitters to receivers. Knowledge receptivity involves receiving knowledge messages so that they can be utilized in practice.[19] This process includes three characteristic ways in which receivers deal with knowledge messages: passive reception, amplification, and transformation.

Passive Reception

Passive reception is the simple act of receiving knowledge messages, with no attempt made by the receiver to seek other pertinent communications or to adapt the knowledge to his practice. (It is to be noted in this presentation that the term, "receiver," may refer to individuals, groups, and / or organizations.) The social worker may receive the knowledge message from one channel, such as an oral report from a social researcher. When the communication is easily understandable and directly related to the receiver's practice, the knowledge is more usable. However, if the knowledge is not ready for use, the receiver might not seek other channels of information or attempt to translate the knowledge so that it could be potentially useful. In essence, the burden is placed on the social researcher to produce specific knowledge, usually in the form of practice prescriptions or proscriptions, for immediate use. Even then, the social worker may not use the knowledge unless he is open to change, a necessary attribute for receiving knowledge and for being willing to implement it. Obviously, the social work practitioner who believes that he does not need any new information to improve his practice is less likely to employ new knowledge than the social worker who is sometimes discouraged because he sees so little progress in his work. Thus, passive reception includes the notions of receiving knowledge that is in a form for immediate use and of the willingness of the receiver to attempt to implement that knowledge.

Amplification

Amplification refers to the active efforts of the receiver to seek clarifications of communications so that they are understandable. While the passive receiver would "turn off" or "tune out" communications that are not clear and directly pertinent to practice, the amplifier would either contact the transmission source or seek other channels which provide expansions and clarifications of the knowledge messages. For example, a social caseworker may read, in a professional journal, about the effectiveness of Rogerian therapy. The research may indicate that the therapy is particularly effective with middle-class college students; however, the process of Rogerian therapy is not clearly communicated. The amplifier may seek clarification by writing to the researchers and asking direct questions about Rogerian therapy, by reading other literature which explains the therapy in more detail, by obtaining and listening to taped recordings of Rogerian therapy sessions, and by discussing Rogerian techniques with proponents of that particular system.[20] Having amplified the knowledge messages, the social worker may attempt to utilize that knowledge. But, as in passive reception, the amplifier might only use the knowledge if it is in a form directly applicable to practice and if he is willing to make changes in his work routines. In this process there are cognitive exchanges between researchers and practitioners about the clarification of knowlege; however, practitioners still expect researchers to indicate how the knowledge could be used.

Transformation

Transformation is a process of knowledge reception in which the social worker adapts research knowledge to his practice. After the social worker understands the contents of the communications, he considers their application potential. If the knowledge is relevant but not in a form directly applicable, the social worker attempts to devise procedures so that the knowledge could be converted for use in practice. In this regard, the dimension of accessibility of knowledge is pertinent. The social worker may transform research knowledge by employing the notions of engineerability, strategic value, location value, and analogy—concepts which are suggestive of the potential applications of research knowledge. Thus, the transformer is an active receiver who attempts to utilize research knowledge even when it is not in a form directly applicable to practice. In addition, the transformer may actively seek information sources, some of which may not be directed to social work at all. He may refer to

the literature in the social sciences and other helping professions, and he may attempt to derive practice principles from that
literature.[21] For example, an administrator of a child welfare
agency may be aware of research results indicating that attitudes
about social issues can be influenced when persons do not have
strong feelings about those issues.[22] The knowledge may have
been obtained from laboratory experiments in social psychology,
and it may not appear to be adaptable to social work. However,
the administrator may transform that knowledge into potential
use by hypothesizing that his educational efforts might be successful if they are directed to community groups that have not
been aware of issues which are of concern to him, e.g., the provision of temporary foster homes for runaway children. Therefore,
newspaper advertising, TV programs, and personal presentations
pertaining to the need and the desirability of temporary foster
homes are arranged for the public and for special interest groups
such as parent-teacher organizations, churches, and service
clubs—organizations which may not be aware of the issue, and
which may be influenced to suggest or to provide resources for
temporary foster homes.

VALUE CONSONANCE

Value refers to "any aspect of a situation, event, or object that
is invested with a preferential interest as being 'good,' 'bad,'
'desirable,' 'undesirable,' or the like." [23] For example, it may be
preferable that all individuals have a right to gain access to opportunity structures within society. Social workers have values
which are reflective of their individual beliefs, of the agencies in
which they work, and of the social work profession.

Value consonance is the extent to which knowledge from social research is compatible with the value structure of the potential user of that knowledge. For example, it may be shown that
"brainwashing" can lead to changes in behaviors and in attitudes; however, such knowledge may not be used by the social
work practitioner who does not advocate using procedures potentially harmful to his clientele. To illustrate further, some social caseworkers may be more prone to use knowledge from

learning theory that is based on rewards rather than on punishments; rewards may be regarded as desirable, while punishments may be regarded as undesirable.

Intertwined with values are the ethical positions of researchers and practitioners about using knowledge. Social researchers should not transmit information which violates their ethical stances and, correspondingly, social work practitioners would not employ knowledge which would be discrepant with their ethical positions. Social researchers usually follow certain procedures to assure research subjects of the confidentiality of their participation in research.[24] Research subjects are informed of the research prior to its conduct, voluntary cooperation is elicited, and the participants are assured that their names will not be identified in the transmission of research results. That is, social researchers adhere to a code of ethics in producing research knowledge.[25] Nevertheless, it is possible that the rights of individuals who participate in research could be violated, especially when the potential user of that knowledge receives research results that identify individual subjects. For example, an executive of an organization may receive the results of a study that was conducted in his organization. The purpose of the research may have been to determine the relationship of supervisory styles to the performances of supervisees. The findings may indicate that one style of supervision is more likely to lead to low productivity than other styles. Moreover, the executive may be able to identify which supervisors are associated with the supervisory style that is least productive and, as a result of such identifications, he may seek to fire, demote, or castigate those supervisors. Many persons would not use that kind of knowledge because it may be in violation of their ethical position regarding the individual's rights to confidentiality—particularly if the individual participated in the research on a voluntary basis.

It is important to note that on specific issues, different ethical positions may be fostered. Social researchers may disagree among themselves about whether subjects should be deceived when research is being conducted.[26] Some social workers may believe that electroshock therapy should not be used because of its potential harm, while others may believe that the potential benefits outweigh the potential harm. The fundamental principle involved here, however, is that the potential user is not likely to employ knowledge if it is discrepant with his ethical positions.

The value systems of key persons in the social agency, the sponsors of that agency, and the agency's clientele may facilitate or impede the use of knowledge. A group worker may believe research results which suggest that marathon encounters are desirable, whereas his agency director and other decision-making persons in the social agency (a residential treatment center) *may not;* hence, the information would not be used. Community organizers may believe that it is worthwhile to use organization strategies such as rent strikes, whereas the client group may not. Or the social caseworker may feel that it is preferable to dispense knowledge about birth control devices, while a client group of low-income Catholics may not because of their definitions and values of human life. Thus, knowledge from social research may or may not be used as a function of its compatibility with the values of social work practitioners and, in addition, its consistency with the values of the client group with whom the practitioners are working.

CAPABILITY FOR IMPLEMENTATION

Capability for implementation refers to the extent to which social workers can actually implement substantive knowledge from social research in their practice.[27] There are six interrelated aspects of this criterion which should be considered by knowledge-users: decision-making power, timing, resources, coordination, workability, and rewards.

Decision-making power is the extent to which the persons who are instrumental for making decisions that affect social work practice will make decisions to implement knowledge from social research. A potential user of knowledge should either be able to make the decision to implement research findings, or he should have access to persons who do have decision-making power; in the final analysis, the application of new knowledge depends on the willingness of decision-makers to call for its implementation. For example, a social caseworker in a family service agency may have confidence in research findings which suggest that accurate assessments of communication difficulties in married couples can be made with the aid of an electronic device for closely monitoring communication interactions.[28] The agency administrator may be less confident about that knowledge, and he may believe less emphasis should be placed on marital counseling. Moreover, he may recognize that the agency's board of directors is reluctant to provide funds for new programs or techniques, and therefore he is unwilling to give a high priority to the establishment of an electronic device in his agency.

Timing refers to the extent to which the reception of knowledge is coincident with the knowledge needs of the individual or organization. Many decisions within social agencies have to be made within a specified period of time; often "as soon as possible," or "as late as yesterday." For example, a group work agency may be able to receive funds from a federal granting agency to establish a program of rehabilitation for teenage drug addicts but, in order to do so, the agency must have knowledge about the incidence and prevalence of drug addiction among teenagers who live in the geographical area covered by the agency. If that knowledge is available, it can be immediately used for establishing eligibility for the program and for a justification of the agency to receive federal funds. The knowledge could be obtained through survey procedures, but the time it takes to conduct the survey may be insufficient to meet deadlines which might have been imposed by the granting agency. Hence, the knowledge would not be used because of improper timing.

Another example of the importance of timing is concerned with the application of knowledge about the use of group techniques by caseworkers in a public assistance agency. Let us assume that the staff of an agency is desirous of seeing more clients and is considering the possibility of shifting from individual to group counseling. The staff of that agency would probably be receptive to knowledge about the relative efficacy of individual and group techniques, and that knowledge might be implemented because it is coincident with the knowledge needs of the staff.

To implement knowledge, the necessary resources must be available. Resources include the availability of financial costs, manpower, time, and equipment. The cost involved in implementing knowledge is obviously an important consideration for decision-makers. A costly item might be the introduction of a computerized system for monitoring the number of agency contacts made by clients, while a less costly item would be the use of check lists as an alternative to process recordings. Even though money might be available, the knowledge may not be implemented. The agency may not have staff who are familiar enough with the new knowledge to employ it immediately. This may necessitate staff training, the use of consultants who are familiar with the knowledge, and / or the hiring of persons who can directly use the knowledge—all of which are resources which may be necessary for the implementation of knowledge.

Coordination refers to the extent to which knowledge-users coordinate their efforts in applying knowledge. This criterion is most salient when several persons are attempting to implement knowledge within an organization. If there is no coordination, it is possible that staff conflict could result from competing usages of the knowledge. Suppose, for example, that in a community organization program, there are several community organizers who have the same goals and are using the same strategy—promoting consensus among different neighborhood groups. Suppose further that research findings suggest that a conflict strategy may lead to social change in neighborhoods; half of the community organizers decide to change to the new approach, while the other half continues to use a consensus strategy. Most of the community organizers may come into contact with people representing the same groups and organizations. If they do, they may be working at cross purposes with each other. Efforts made by organizers to promote consensus may be undermined by the efforts of other organizers to foster conflict. Thus, not only might staff conflict appear, but also there is an inconsistent implementation of knowledge.

Workability refers to the extent to which the knowledge "works" in practice. Because research knowledge is often obtained from situations other than that of the specific work situation in which the social worker is engaged, it usually must be modified or adapted. In view of this, the knowledge that is implemented is often in the form of hypotheses. These hypotheses can be tried in practice, but some means should be built-in so that the practitioner can assess the extent to which the knowledge appears to be useful.

For example, a social agency may employ case aides who are from a low-income client group. The purpose of their employment might be to provide more appropriate services to low-income clients. It might have been hypothesized that this could be accomplished by the use of case aides because research findings suggest that clients are more willing to discuss their needs with persons with whom they can closely identify. In the specific context of the agency it might have turned out that no more clients were contacted than were seen before the use of case aides. Moreover, additional services may not have been provided to the low-income group. It might have been possible, for example, that the case aides were regarded as "sell-outs" to the "establishment"; and the case aides may also have aroused feelings of resentment in other low-income persons who would have preferred to be hired as case aides themselves. As a result of this information, it may be decided that the agency's use of case aides is not justifiable. The point made here is that practitioners should make judgments about the workability of research knowledge so they can decide whether or not its use should be continued, modified, or discontinued.

Finally, it is believed that social workers are more likely to implement research findings when they are rewarded for their efforts. Rewards may come in terms of individual satisfaction in working, in making changes which provide better services to clientele, and in learning about available knowledge that could improve one's practice. The social worker may receive his rewards through committee work in professional organizations, by lecturing to various groups, or by initiating social reforms. For example, a social work practitioner may be convinced that present abortion laws are inadequate, and he may be confident in research findings about the psychological and social harm that is often inflicted on persons who either have illegitimate children or illegal abortions. Hence, he may advocate for legalized abortion, and his efforts in that type of social action may be rewarding for him.

Within the social agency where the practitioner works, the rewards could appear in the form of recognition which may lead to pay increases, promotions, time off to attend conferences, and so forth. Certainly, the social worker is unlikely to attempt to use research findings if he receives little encouragement for his efforts, or if he is chastised because he is not doing other things which have higher priority for the social agency.

A Rating System for Using Research Results

The criteria for applying the results of social research can be used to determine the implementation potential of research knowledge in social work practice. The rating procedure below serves two purposes: 1) to briefly summarize dimensions for considering the implementation of findings from social research; and 2) to serve as a tentative device by which potential knowledge-users might be able to systematize their thoughts regarding implementation.

Referring to Table 2 it is seen that the categories for rating are "yes," "potentially yes," "probably not," and "no." Moreover, it is noted that the dimension of confidence in knowledge is not included among the questions. This is because a separate rating system was provided earlier for making confidence judgments. In addition, it is believed that one should not attempt to consider implementing knowledge unless he is confident in it. Thus, the questions in Table 2 pertain to the implementation of *sound* research knowledge, i.e., knowledge of which one has moderate or high degrees of confidence.

Table 2
Criteria for Implementing Knowledge

	Yes	Potentially Yes	Probably Not	No
Is the knowledge relevant?				
Is the knowledge accessible?				
Are the potential users receptive to the knowledge?				
Are the value systems of the potential users consonant with the knowledge?				
Do the potential users have the capability for implementing the knowledge?				

In order to use these questions, one would determine whether or not the criteria for implementing knowledge can be satisfied. Turning to the example of the process of using research results at the beginning of this chapter, it is evident that Miss U. would answer "yes" to the five questions. Having assured herself that she was confident in the knowledge, she believed it was relevant and accessible for use. She was receptive, she believed the knowledge was consonant with her system of values, and the school system in which she worked was capable of implementing the research results.

If all the questions are answered affirmatively, one should implement research results; on the other hand, if all of the questions are answered negatively, there are probably too many barriers for knowledge implementation. When the questions are answered "potentially yes" or "probably not," it is an indication that there should probably be more thought and discussion about the implementation of research findings.

Chapter 4

~.

Using Social
Research Methods

Methodological knowledge refers to the strategies and observational techniques of social research, i.e., to research methods which can be employed to generate substantive knowledge. This type of knowledge is usually transmitted by researchers, and received by other researchers interested in finding better methods for securing valid information from social research investigations. Thomas, for example, indicates that the methods of research employed in the behavioral sciences can be used for research on the problems and issues of social work.[1] However, methodological knowledge, or research methods, can also be used for providing information to social workers as an aid for the conduct of social work practice.[2] The use of social research methods for practice is based on these primary considerations: 1) Since social research methods are tools for gathering systematic information about social phenomena, they can be regarded as methods for information processing; 2) The conduct of social work practice requires that the practitioner obtain and process information about the clients, groups, organizations, or communities with whom he works; 3) Social research methods can be used, or adapted for use, to serve as information processing tools for social work practice.

These themes will be developed in this chapter, which is organized into several interrelated areas: the need for the practitioner's use of research methods—more specifically, basic preconditions regarding the use of information-processing techniques; a section devoted to dimensions which can affect the social worker's selection of research methods; the model of social work practice as a problem-solving process, and its analogy to the research process—the purpose of which is to present a scheme for locating research methods that can be employed in various components of social work practice; suggested uses of social research methods.

Preconditions for Using
Social Research Methods

In order to receive communications about social research methods—either as a passive receiver, amplifier, or transformer —three preconditions should be fulfilled: 1) The social worker identifies his information needs, and is desirous of obtaining information to meet those needs; 2) The social worker does not have adequate information-processing methods to secure the desired information; 3) The social worker believes that research methods can be adapted for use in social work practice.

INFORMATION NEEDS OF SOCIAL
WORK PRACTITIONERS

Social work practitioners need information directly related to the tasks and functions in which they are engaged. The social planner and community organizer require information about the social and health needs of a community and the available resources for meeting those needs. The social caseworker uses information about the potential problems of his clients, such as their social functioning at home and at work, their financial resources and living conditions, and their states of physical and mental health. That is, social caseworkers need information for making appraisals of their clients' needs and problems so they can develop and implement appropriate treatment goals. A social group worker may institute a series of group discussions on drug abuse with a group of teenagers for the purpose of communicating knowledge about drugs and changing the attitudes of those teenagers. Certainly, he needs to know about the attitudes and beliefs of his group members about drugs. Moreover, he might be interested in whether the group is acquiring knowledge and changing its attitudes as a result of the group discussions. Hence, an important consideration in the social worker's use of research methods is his information needs for practice. But, he must not only need the information, he must also want it—i.e., he should actively attempt to secure the information he needs.

In addition to acquiring information related to the conduct of practice with social work clientele, the social worker may also wish to communicate information about his practice to other persons and organizations. The social caseworker may present information about specific aspects of his work to a consulting psychiatrist, psychologist, or some other specialist. His presentation may include qualitative and quantitative descriptions of a specific case (or cases), for example, the number of interviews that a client missed, the attitudes of the client toward authority figures, the client's functioning on his job, facts about the client's living circumstances, the caseworker's relationship with the client, and so forth. The administrator may want to communicate to his staff his efforts (and his successes and failures) in attempting to secure increased funds and expanded programs from the agency's board of directors and other sponsoring bodies. He might include the ways in which he attempted to justify the expansion of the agency in terms of information regarding staff capability and the progress of the agency in helping individuals and groups. The group worker may need to present information to his supervisor about the nature and extent of his activities with the numbers and types of groups he is working with and his progress in articulating and achieving group goals. The community organizer may communicate to the members of a welfare rights organization the extent to which its membership has expanded, the impact it has had on the local welfare department, and so forth. In all of the above efforts in communication by social workers, it is necessary that observations and experiences be organized and summarized in a format which includes generalized descriptions, simple facts, and inferences based on those descriptions and facts.

Closely related to the communication of information about the activities and progress of social workers in accomplishing and in obtaining advice on how to accomplish specific tasks is the desire for providing information pertaining to social work accountability, i.e., the extent to which social agencies report on their overall efforts, effectiveness, and efficiency to groups they are accountable to. The director of a day care center may receive funds from a federal granting agency. The day care center may be housed in an elementary school setting and be geared to provide day care facilities for low-income families so that the mothers can seek employment while their children are being cared for. Within the center there may be a staff of teachers, social workers, and nonprofessional volunteers. The director is accountable for the money spent in the program and for the accomplishment of program objectives. Interested groups are not only the program sponsors, but also the mothers in the program, other low-income persons who are potentially eligible for the program, etc. To be accountable to those groups the director has to obtain and process information about program activities, costs, efficiency, and progress; and adaptations of evaluative techniques such as monitoring, cost analytic and survey methods may be useful to him.[3]

If the practicing social worker is cognizant of his information needs (in relation to accountability, the conduct of his practice, or the communication of information about specific tasks to other persons and organizations) and he desires to secure the necessary information, the first precondition for selecting research methods as an aid to practice is fulfilled. Obviously, if information is not required or deemed necessary, there is no need for the practitioner to select research methods.

INADEQUATE INFORMATION-PROCESSING METHODS

A second precondition for receiving communications about research methods is the practitioner's recognition or belief that his existing procedures for securing information are inadequate. The procedures may be inadequate in that they are too time-consuming, inaccurate, inefficient, or simply not in use, i.e., practitioners may not be aware of available procedures for securing information necessary for their work. On the other hand, if the social worker believes that he effectively gathers information, he is not likely to want to receive or to seek communications about research methods. For example, an administrator may have up-to-date knowledge about his agency's operations, the group worker may have an adequate system for assessing the needs of group members and for structuring groups, and the social planner may employ satisfactory indices of need by which he can describe the extent to which new facilities should be planned and old programs modified or abolished.

Information-processing procedures might be regarded as adequate by social workers, but as inadequate by sponsors of social work programs. In such instances, social workers may be pressured to seek those information-processing methods which would satisfy the sponsors of their programs. For example, a program sponsor may desire quantitative (rather than qualitative) information about the relative costs of social services with respect to the amounts of service that have been rendered to specific types of clientele. Although the administrator and the program staff may have believed that their existing information system (which did not include the above type of information) was adequate, they may be forced to comply with the sponsor's requests—particularly, if the sponsor may have the power to abolish the program if the staff does not provide such information. Thus, social workers may come to believe that their information-processing system is "inadequate" by means of persons and organizations having direct influence over their program operations.

BELIEF IN THE ADAPTABILITY OF RESEARCH METHODS

In order to seek and to receive communications about research methods, social workers should also believe that those methods can be adapted for use in practice. It is unlikely that one would look for research methods as possible procedures for processing practice information if he regards research methods as useful *only* for the conduct of research investigations.

The social planner who conducts surveys of needs and resources, develops indices, and analyzes social trends over time, incorporates research methods in his practice.[4] Similarly, the behavioral therapist who approaches the management of cases and groups from an experimental point of view utilizes research methods.[5] Practitioners who already incorporate research methods are more likely to be receptive to communications about other research methods that might be useful. In contrast, social workers who do not use research methods as information-processing techniques are less likely to be open to such communications. In essence, the more experience one has in using research methods for social work practice, the more likely is it that he will seek and be receptive to the further use of those methods.

It should be pointed out, however, that some practitioners may incorporate research methods without being aware of it. For example, questionnaires might be employed by group workers to gain information from their clients regarding their progress in achieving individual goals. Although the group workers use an observational technique—i.e., questionnaires—from social research, they may not identify it as a research method, possibly because of a mistaken assumption that research methods can be used *only* in formal research investigations. To illustrate this point further, the behavioral therapist may regard his observational procedures as simply practice procedures, not understanding that those procedures are, in part, derived and adapted from the technology of social research. Thus, the social work practitioner is more likely to receive communications about research methods if he can identify his use of those methods in his work.

Dimensions Affecting the Use of Social Research Methods

There are five interrelated dimensions which can affect the social work practitioner's use of research methods. These are the availability of research methods, the correspondence of those methods to the information requirements of practitioners, the compatibility of those methods with the social worker's practice, the extent to which those methods can be implemented, and their costs.

AVAILABILITY OF RESEARCH METHODS

As indicated in chapter 1, social research methods include strategies, observational techniques, and analytic procedures for gathering and processing information about social phenomena. These methods are available when practitioners are able to locate communication sources describing them in sufficient detail so that they can be implemented. The primary source of communication is the literature, but other sources such as research centers, conferences, workshops, consultations, and correspondence can be used.

The classic sources of research methods in the literature are in research text books and books of readings. Some texts are written primarily for students of research, but also include generalized descriptions of research principles which can be adapted to practice.[6] Many research books focus on specific phenomena more related to the tasks and functions of social workers.[7] In addition, there are books which deal exclusively with particular techniques and modes of inquiry,[8] and others which contain a great deal of information about data collection instruments.[9]

Other sources of discussions about the use of research methods are in articles and papers in the literature of the helping professions and the social sciences. Furthermore, articles reporting the results of research studies often include the research instruments used to process information; e.g., rating scales, classification systems, questionnaires, psychological tests, etc. They can be located in references such as *Medicus Indicus, Abstracts for Social Workers, Psychological Abstracts,* and *Sociological Abstracts;* and in a variety of journals: *Social Work, American Psychologist, Social Casework, Social Service Review, Child Welfare, Journal of Applied Behavioral Analysis, Journal of Personality and Social Psychology, Psychiatry, Public Interest, Daedalus, American Journal of Public Health, Psychometrika, Sociometry, American Journal of Orthopsychiatry, Welfare in Review, Federal Probation, Journal of Research in Crime and Delinquency,* and *Annals of the American Academy of Political and Social Science.*

It is important to note that the bulk of the literature about research methods is addressed to social researchers, and not specifically to social work practitioners. Social workers are more apt to read about research methods included in literature devoted to the specification of techniques that can be employed in practice. This is because the research methods presented in the literature dealing with practice interventions are already adapted for use, whereas research methods in the literature not especially devoted to practice may need to be modified and adapted before they can be used. Examples of topics in the practice literature (i.e., literature in social work and related professions pertaining to the tasks and functions of social caseworkers, group workers, administrators, community organizers, and policy developers) are the use of the Planning-Programming-Budgeting-System (PBBS) for administrative analysts,[10] the assessment of self concept by employing research methods used for studying the effectiveness of Rogerian Therapy,[11] the determination of progress in clients and their families by using movement scales and family functioning scales,[12] the use of classification systems of diagnosis and treatment,[13] the application of learning principles for changing complex human behaviors,[14] devices for obtaining feedback in group work,[15] the coordination of statistical reporting in social agencies,[16] and the community representativeness of social agency clientele.[17]

Literature pertaining to research methods is also available from research centers in the form of bulletins, pamphlets, monographs, and books. Research centers may be under the auspices of local, state, and federal governments, universities, or private organizations, e.g., the Research Department of the California Youth Authority, Research Divisions of the National Institutes of Health, the Bureau of Applied Social Research at Columbia University, the Institute of Social Research at the University of Michigan, the Department of Research and Evaluation of the Community Service Society in New York City. These organizations will provide copies of questionnaires, interview schedules, and other data collection devices that have been employed in research studies, and which may be useful for practice. Although the specific observational techniques that are available may not be tailor-made for one's specific practice concerns, they may be modifiable. For example, the administrator who needs to determine the extent of drug usage in the clients who are processed through his social agency may locate questionnaires on drug usage. The specific questions may not be geared to the population with which he is concerned; however, the items in the questionnaires serve as examples—and that information plus available principles for questionnaire construction may facilitate the administrator's development of a new questionnaire for his purposes.

In addition to the literature, one can also locate social researchers who may provide consultation regarding the use of research methods. Researchers will correspond with interested persons, and provide more detailed information about the procedures they have employed; they may be able to assist in modifying instruments so that they are more suitable for deriving information of immediate use to the practitioners. Moreover, conferences and workshops may be held, typically in professional organizations, which are addressed to the use of research methods; e.g., workshops on developing indices of poverty and social need, the employment of computer systems for processing checks to welfare recipients, and procedures for efficient cost accounting are topics of interest to administrators and social planners.

In summary, then, there is a variety of sources on research methods, many of which might be usable in social work practice. The problem, as viewed here, is not so much one of availability; it is, instead, one in which social work students and practitioners are not taught to seek research methods for use in practice. Furthermore, researchers do not typically communicate methodological knowledge with the objective of presenting it so that it can be used by practitioners. This makes the role of social workers as receivers of communications more difficult, for they must be *amplifiers* and *transformers* of such communications rather than simply being *passive receivers*. Nevertheless, it is the thesis of this chapter that the search for research methods as tools for practice may be profitable, and it is the intent herein to provide suggestions which may aid in this search.

INFORMATION CORRESPONDENCE

An important dimension related to the social work practitioner's use of research methods is information correspondence, i.e., the extent to which the research methods correspond to the social worker's information requirements. Research methods have information correspondence when they can be used to provide desired information that pertains to the specific tasks and functions of social work, i.e., diagnosis or assessment, choosing among alternative intervention strategies, describing program efforts and progress, furnishing staff members with follow-up information about the results of the intervention activities, and so forth.

Social caseworkers in a family service agency may be interested in following the progress of clients who have terminated from the agency. Procedures related to techniques of research interviewing are useful for obtaining information such as the clients' perceptions of their current social functioning and the benefits (or lack of benefits) they have received from social caseworkers.

However, those procedures may or may not correspond to the agency's information needs because of the amount of time necessary for gathering and processing the information. The social caseworkers may need to have the information in a short period of time for the purpose of planning new agency priorities. The use of sampling plus telephone interviewing could be sufficient for the agency's purposes; e.g., a simple random sample of 50 clients may be chosen from a list of 200 clients who have terminated in the past year, and those clients in the sample could be called and engaged in brief telephone interviews.[18]

Program directors who are interested in evaluation may not want to adopt a wide range of evaluative techniques, but they may use techniques of questionnaire construction and cost accounting to develop forms pertaining to information they require for program budgeting, e.g., expenditures in relation to the amount, duration, and type of services provided to their clients.[19]

Community organizers in social action projects may need to know why two or more strategies work or do not work in different circumstances of practice. Questionnaires for determining perceptions of community issues might produce interesting information, but such information may not correspond with the immediate needs of the community organizers. Compilations of narrative accounts of the community organizers' interventions and the specification of which interventions were used in which circumstances may be desirable as a way to provide information which suggests what strategies appear to work.[20] If the funds, time, and motivation are present, the community organizers may attempt to employ an experiment for comparing the relative efficacy of two or more strategies in two contrasting practice situations.[21] For example, conflict and consensus strategies may be used in an attempt to organize persons in neighborhoods characterized as representing different ethnic groups; and the community organizers would gather information about the successes and failures of the strategies, from their own perspectives and from the perspectives of the people with whom they have come in contact.

METHOD COMPATIBILITY

Method compatibility is determined by the extent to which the knowledge and values necessary to employ the research methods are compatible with the knowledge and value structures of social workers. The knowledge required to use the research method should not be so complex that it would take an extraordinary amount of time for the social worker to comprehend it. For example, the research method may require a knowledge of computer programming based on mathematical models. The typical social worker would not understand such a method without a translation of basic concepts into terms compatible with his practice. The time that it takes the social worker (who is not a research or statistical expert) to learn the necessary principles for implementing the method may simply be too expensive, particularly if it is not clear how the method could be specifically used in practice.

Although the knowledge required to use research methods may not be too complex, it still may not correspond to the social worker's knowledge structure, i.e., the way in which he organizes his concepts for viewing his practice activities. For example, there may be an available method for assessing the potential reinforcers in a client's environment. Such an assessment method might be useful for behavioral therapists; however, it may not be useful to social workers who have no knowledge of learning principles or the techniques of behavior modification. Unless the social worker makes a commitment to be willing to change his notions of practice and to learn other concepts and principles, he would not regard that particular assessment instrument as useful.

Some research methods may require that observations be made without the subject's being aware of it. For example, a one-way viewing screen may be used to observe interactions in groups and families. However, the social worker (or even the social researcher) may have a value structure (i.e., the way in which he organizes his values for conducting practice) which is incompatible with using such a device. The use of a one-way viewing screen might be regarded as permissible only if the family or group consents to its use. Families may refuse to be observed in that manner, and that would be binding on the social worker who might regard the use of the procedure as unethical without the informed consent of the family members.

Other social research methods may involve the use of deception.[22] Social psychological research investigations often use a confederate, i.e., another person who feigns ignorance of the research but who is, in fact, associated with it. For example, a group worker could use a confederate in assisting him to make an assessment of group functioning. A confederate enters into a group meeting; and he shouts, screams, and is antagonistic to the group worker and the group. The group worker then studies the group reactions and interactions in relation to the intruder (the confederate) to assess the extent of group cohesion under stress. This procedure could be regarded as extreme and antithetical to the group worker's underlying values about self-determination and undue manipulation; thus, he would regard the method as not useful because it is incompatible with his value-structure.

IMPLEMENTATION OF RESEARCH METHODS

Implementation refers to the extent to which research methods could be directly or indirectly used by social workers. A research method is directly useful when it can be employed without any modification in format and procedures. In contrast, a research method that is indirectly useful is one that requires changes so that it can be adapted to social work practice. In general, principles of research design, sampling, and instrument construction are indirectly useful; while specific data gathering instruments—such as standardized questionnaires, rating scales, psychological tests, observational coding systems and interview schedules—may be either directly or indirectly useful.

Suppose that a survey of housing needs and resources was conducted by a team of social researchers. A questionnaire may have been used as the primary technique for gathering data. Let us further suppose that a local planning commission (in a different community from the one in which the survey was conducted) is

considering whether an expansion of multiple occupancy dwellings is necessary, and in that regard it would like to have the
opinions of middle-income residents in a particular neighborhood. The questionnaire employed by the social researchers
may have included a number of items addressed to middle-income residents about their housing needs and preferences, as
well as their attitudes and opinions about the necessity for multiple occupancy dwellings. The social planners in the planning
commission may have access to the questionnaire, and they may
believe that the items tap opinions about multiple occupancy
dwellings. Moreover, since the research questionnaire was constructed for use on the same type of population (middle-income
residents) in which the social planners are interested, it may be
decided that the questionnaire can be directly used. Factors that
favor direct usage are the appropriateness of language and word-
ing for the persons to be queried, the willingness and ability of
persons to respond to those types of questions, and the relevance
of the items to the interests of the practitioner.

In contrast, suppose that the planning commission is concerned about housing needs and preferences for another neighborhood in the community, which is comprised of a large number of Italian immigrants. The questionnaire used in the social
research survey is in English, and the immigrants' knowledge of
English may be slight; in addition, they may not understand the
syntax and construction of words used by social researchers. The
questionnaire could not be directly used, but it might be modified and adapted for use. It might be changed into an interview
schedule—which contains a translation of the items into Italian,
and which includes additional items pertaining to the immigrants' living styles in Italy and their desired living styles in
the United States. The questionnaire is indirectly used in that it
forms the basis for the development of an interview schedule
which is constructed by translating pertinent items from the
questionnaire and by developing additional items that could be
employed in face-to-face interviews. The social planners would
have chosen face-to-face interviewing because the immigrant
population is predominantly low income and has little profi-

ciency in English—factors which do not favor the return of mailed questionnaires.

Another example of implementation pertains to the needs of a group worker for analyzing group interaction. The group worker might use Bales' Interaction Process Analysis, which involves the use of one or more observers who count frequencies of behavior for each of the group members.[23] Categories for observation are as follows: shows solidarity, shows tension release, agrees, gives suggestion, gives opinion, gives orientation, asks for orientation, asks for opinion, asks for suggestion, disagrees, shows tension, and shows antagonism. These categories may be directly used by the group worker who desires an assessment of the extent and type of interaction in his group. However, the group worker may not want to have other persons observing his group for the purpose of counting interaction behaviors; and he may be interested in a smaller number of categories that he regards as more important, e.g., spontaneity in discussion, or the emission of positive or negative verbal reinforcements. The group worker could seek other interaction coding systems, or he could use Bales' system indirectly. For example, he might tape record the group sessions and analyze verbal responses in relation to some of the categories above and to additional dimensions of interest.

COSTS

When new procedures are introduced in social work practice for processing information, the costs may rise considerably. Social workers who plan to use research methods must consider the extent to which they are willing and able to afford the primary and secondary costs necessary for implementing social research methods. Primary costs are those that refer to direct financial costs in terms of money, equipment, purchase of supplies, office facilities, and so forth; while secondary costs involve the use of manpower and facilities which could detract from the social worker's primary function of direct service, e.g., time required in filling out forms, devising questionnaires, and analyzing responses for assessment purposes.[24]

The social worker can make cost estimates by considering the financial outlay necessary for implementing the research methods; the extent of manpower, time, and agency resources that need to be provided; and the potential savings that might result. For example, the use of a brief questionnaire for assessing selected client problems may require the following costs: $50 in supplies and 15 minutes of the caseworker's time with each new case. The costs are relatively slight and, in addition, the employment of that device might result in substantial savings—the questionnaire may serve as a substitute for detailed process-recording and may also reduce interviewing time. In contrast, an extensive interview schedule which contains a variety of information and requires two hours for each interview may be too costly. It may only add to the existing burden that practitioners have in their daily work and, in particular, if the information is collected without being utilized, it would be a wasteful procedure.

Selecting Social Research Methods

Social work practitioners, for the most part, are not accustomed to regard social research methods as potentially useful in their work. Because of this, it is desirable to formulate a plan which may assist the practitioner in selecting research methods. The scheme presented in this section is based on two assumptions: 1) Practitioners are more likely to be sensitized to selecting research methods when they understand the similarities between components of practice and of research; 2) A delineation of the practice-research analogy can serve as a conceptual device for locating research methods which can be utilized in social work practice.

THE PRACTICE-RESEARCH ANALOGY

All of social work practice cannot be easily categorized into a simple model because of its various subdisciplines having different tasks and functions, its eclectic nature in using theoretical frameworks from other helping professions and the social sciences, and its use in a wide variety of social, health, and educational agencies. The conceptualization of social work practice that appears to depict the widest range of tasks and functions is that of the problem-solving model.[25] This includes five interrelated components: assessment, formulation of intervention plans, implementation of intervention, evaluations of progress, and termination.[26] These components of practice can be employed to represent much of the work conducted by social caseworkers, group workers, community organizers, administrators, and policy developers.[27] Correspondingly, social research is complex, and one model cannot delineate all types of social research activities. Nevertheless, the problem-solving model is also useful for conceptualizing the process of social research.[28] The components of the research process are problem formulation, research strategy and sampling, implementation of research strategy and data collection, analyses of data, and conclusions and interpretations.

The problem-solving models of social work practice and social research are based on the scientific method, and the components of these models can be regarded as analogous.[29] In Table 3, the research analogues of each of the five practice components are included in the same rows. Thus, "problem formulation" is analogous to "assessment" in row 1; "research strategy and sampling," to "formulation of intervention plans" in row 2; etc. Prior to discussing each of the five analogues, it should be pointed out

Table 3
Components of Problem-Solving Models for Practice and Research

Practice	Research
1. Assessment	Problem formulation
2. Formulation of intervention plans	Research strategy and sampling
3. Implementation of intervention	Implementation of research strategy and data collection
4. Evaluations of progress	Analyses of data
5. Termination	Conclusions and interpretations

that the components in practice are interrelated (e.g., assessment or reassessment may occur while the worker is implementing his intervention plans), as are the components in research (e.g., conclusions about data may relate to the alternatives that are considered for study in problem formulation). Thus, for purposes of simplicity, a step-by-step process in both practice and research is assumed. Moreover, this presentation is focused on those components most directly analogous, i.e., those which are indicated in Table 3—although it should be noted that more than one component of research may be related to a practice component; e.g., problem formulation, data collection, and analyses of data could all relate to assessment.

Assessment and Problem Formulation

Assessment and problem formulation are focused on the specification of problems that need to be solved, so that the researcher can develop appropriate research strategies and observational techniques; it is important for practitioners so they can formulate desirable intervention plans.

The procedures involved in problem formulation are conceptualization of the problem, the articulation of researchable hypotheses, the operationalization of concepts, conceptual clarification, and a determination of the feasibility of the research based on available data. These procedures have been discussed in chapters 1 and 2, where it was indicated that the social researcher often formulates research problems in the context of social interactions with other persons and groups.

Assessment is essentially a determination by the social worker and his clientele of whether there is a problem and what the nature of that problem is. The community organizer, for example, may be interested in organizing minority group members of a community for the purpose of achieving a system by which local government officials are responsive to their needs. Prior to the formulation of intervention strategies, the community organizer makes an assessment of the community, i.e., the extent and type of community leadership, the degree to which government officials are responsive to minority groups, the nature and extent of minority group populations, the current and past experiences of minority group persons in dealing with government officials, and so forth.

An administrator may be interested in reorganizing the structure of his agency. Before he plans such a reorganization, he may make an assessment of the existing organization in terms of the extent to which it is efficient in achieving agency goals, and the extent to which it allows for staff participation in decision-making. Thus, the administrator might assess the tasks of his staff members with respect to their services and responsibilities, determining the degree of overlap among staff functions. The purposes of that assessment would be to determine whether there is a need for reorganization and to locate sources of conflict or role strain among staff members.

Social caseworkers and group workers make assessments of the needs and goals of their clients and groups. They consider the clients' requests for help, their difficulties in social, psychological, and economic functioning, their capacities for participating in treatment, their expectations of treatment, their potential contributions to groups, etc. Such information is useful for identifying those problems which can be effectively dealt with through casework or group work interventions.

The social researcher usually has more time than the social work practitioner to formulate problems; hence, he may process the information he obtains in a relatively more systematic manner. In addition, the social researcher poses problems which he attempts to solve by producing information relevant to them—the development of concepts, the formulation and testing of hypotheses. The practitioner poses a problem, gathers information, and utilizes it in providing direct services. Thus, there are some differences between practitioners and social researchers in the amount of time and effort employed to formulate problems. The problem formulation process in research and practice is similar in that concepts are specified, available information is utilized to articulate the problems, and tentative hypotheses are developed.

Formulation of Intervention Plans and
Research Strategies and Sampling

The formulation of intervention plans involves the selection of one or more strategies which might solve the practice problem, while research strategy and sampling involves the selection of research designs and sampling plans necessary to provide evidence for the objectives posed for study. As indicated in chapter 1, research designs are comprised of a combination of three basic strategies: experimentation, survey methods, and case study procedures. Involved in the selection of research strategies and sampling methods is a consideration of which type of strategy is more appropriate and feasible for providing valid information related to the research problem. In addition, planning for desired generalizability of the research results involves a selection of reliable data collection procedures and appropriate sampling methods, which may range from probability sampling to sampling by convenience, i.e., accidental sampling.

Having made an assessment of the social situation and the problems identified for solution, the social work practitioner formulates intervention plans. Such plans are based on the social worker's knowledge of similar problems and situations, the specific problems identified in the assessment, and the means of intervention to deal with those problems.

The social caseworker may have assessed a problem as primarily economic for a family in a crisis situation, e.g., the death of the principal breadwinner, with the family in grief and also bereft of economic sources for living. The social caseworker's intervention plans may be to provide or locate sources of economic assistance for the family and to help it deal with its immediate circumstances, all within the framework of a helping and supportive role.

The community organizer may have made an assessment of the conditions in a housing project in which he found that the tenants were dissatisfied, the housing was below standard, and housing officials were negligent in making necessary repairs in tenants' apartments. Based on that assessment and the tenants' desires to have better housing, the community organizer may formulate plans to organize the tenants to publicize their substandard housing conditions, to confront the housing and city officials with those conditions, and to possibly call for a rent strike.

An administrator of a social agency which is focused on preventing delinquency in teenagers by the use of activity groups and recreational programs may formulate the following intervention plan: emphasis should be placed on drug education and the development of a referral system for teenagers who need help to overcome drug addiction; the agency's activities should be coordinated with the schools and with other agencies in providing drug education for adolescents. The formulation of the general plan may be predicated on the following assessment: the number of teenagers participating in agency activities has declined; many teenagers do not regard activity groups as helpful; many of the teenagers who discontinued agency services are "hooked on drugs"; and the incidence and prevalence of drug addiction among teenagers has increased dramatically.

Both researchers and practitioners devise tentative strategies for solving the problems they have identified. Whether or not those strategies can be implemented depends upon the contingencies which may develop during the conduct of practice or research. In general (and in particular for the employment of experimentation, survey methods, and probability sampling procedures), the use of research strategies requires planning for a systematic collection of data; whereas, social work practitioners need to plan for a greater flexibility in approach, e.g., by planning for two alternative strategies, either of which could be employed in the same practice situation.

Implementation of Intervention and Research Strategy and Data Collection

Implementation of intervention is similar to implementation of research strategy and data collection in these ways: 1) the plans for intervention or research are carried out; 2) observations are made about the practicality of the implementation procedures.

The social work practitioner can be regarded as an experimenter and a participant observer. He is an experimenter in the sense that he uses himself and manipulates other resources to achieve practice goals, while he is a participant observer in that he observes himself in interaction with his clientele and other significant persons or groups. Indeed, one mode of practice uses the analogue of experimentation directly—behavioral modification. In that type of practice, baseline observations of the frequency and duration of behaviors are taken prior to treatment; manipulations are made with respect to the deployment of positive and/or negative reinforcements which are contingent on desirable and undesirable behaviors; and observations are tabulated with respect to the changes in the frequency and duration of baseline behaviors. Correspondingly, experimental procedures are used in social research for studying individual units (persons, groups, or organizations). Moreover, as has been pointed out earlier, one technique of data collection employed in research is that of participant observation—where the observer is in interaction with members of a social system and where he attempts to describe and synthesize such experiences.

Social work practitioners and social researchers are similar in that they both collect information. The practitioner may collect information based on quantitative or qualitative data, e.g., the tape recordings of group sessions by group workers, the production of case summaries by social caseworkers, the documentation of monies expended by administrators, the collection of data from interviews and questionnaires by social planners. However, social researchers typically emphasize the collection of reliable and valid information in order to make generalizations beyond the situation in which research is conducted, while social workers are more interested in the immediate practice situation. Moreover, social researchers usually collect more extensive data for longer periods of time. For example, a field experiment for evaluating the effectiveness of group work may involve the use of experimental and control groups for periods of time ranging up to one or more years, with the recipients of group work services being followed up for several years. In contrast, a group worker may believe that his procedures are not working, and he may switch immediately to an alternate strategy in his next group meeting.

Evaluations of Progress and Analyses of Data

Evaluations of progress are made on the basis of observations in practice, while analyses of data are performed on observations secured through the systematic use of research procedures. Whereas the research data are typically quantified and subject to statistical modes of analysis, observations in practice are often evaluated by the practitioner's judgments. The analyses of data in social research include such objectives as a description of trends in the data, a consideration of the joint relationships among variables and of the possible spuriousness of those relationships, a determination of the extent to which research results can be generalized to larger populations by means of statistical inference, and an abstraction of concepts and hypotheses from qualitative data.

The social work practitioner makes observations in order to form judgments about whether or not his intervention plan is working. The purposes of such an evaluation are to decide when and if alternate strategies should be employed, to plan for termination of social work contact if the problem has been solved or if the available strategies do not appear to be helpful, to plan for referrals to other agencies which may have the necessary resources and means to solve the practice problem. For example, the social caseworker observes whether or not the client is making changes or is able to cope more effectively with his situation, he observes whether the client reports more or less satisfaction with himself and significant others, he may obtain reports of the client's progress from the client's family, job, school, etc., and he forms judgments about the client's degree of involvement in casework and the potential value of such help.

Evaluations of progress may be made *during* the conduct of social work practice. For example, a group worker may attempt to use the techniques of role playing in his group. The group members may not be receptive to the use of that procedure, and this may compel the group worker to reconsider and/or abandon the use of role playing. The analogous situation may also occur in research, where the research subjects may refuse to participate, e.g., in taking I.Q. tests. The researcher would have to form a judgment about either modifying or abolishing that aspect of the research.

Termination and Conclusions and Interpretations

Termination refers to the conscious planning of the social worker to discontinue working with his clientele. It may be a result of problem solution or of the determination that the social work intervention is not helpful. In the event that the social work intervention does not appear to work, the social worker may attempt to appraise the situation and seek consultation regarding different approaches or possible referral sources. Correspondingly, the conclusions and interpretations of a research investigation refer to the researcher's report regarding the accomplishment of his research objectives. If the objectives are not achieved, the researcher may suggest alternate means of study.

In the process of terminating his clientele, the social work practitioner makes conclusions about his interventions, and he may consider the implications of his efforts—with respect to the subsequent progress of his clientele, and with reference to his future work. For example, the social caseworker may seek information about what happens to clients after casework is discontinued. Are the clients functioning adequately in their environments? did they benefit from their experiences with the caseworkers? would the clients seek similar services if other difficulties arise in the future? The group worker may also be interested in information about individuals who terminated from groups. Likewise, the community organizer and administrator make decisions to terminate problem-solving efforts, and follow-up information may be desired about the effectiveness of those endeavors.

The social researcher considers the implications of his findings in relation to what he has learned from the research. Were the research techniques effective in accomplishing the research objectives? Should the study be replicated in order to increase the generalizability of the research results? Are new, substantive, and methodological questions developed from the research?

Of course, clients may discontinue involvement with social work practice, irrespective of the social worker's plans for interventions; and subjects may drop out of a research study prior to its completion. In such instances, there may be a loss of information concerning the progress of social work clientele, and the extent to which social researchers can draw reliable conclusions. Nevertheless, both social researchers and social workers attempt to secure the necessary information for solving the problems which they have posed for solution. Perhaps, the fundamental difference between social work practice and social research stems from the different relationships among social workers and their clientele, as compared with social researchers and their research subjects. While the social worker seeks to help his clientele, and gathers information toward that end, the social researcher seeks help *from* his research subjects to provide him with information related to the production of knowledge. Hence, social workers seek more immediate information which can be used in the specific practice situation and, in contrast, social researchers seek information for making adequate generalizations with respect to their knowledge objectives.

A SELECTION PLAN

To facilitate the selection of research methods which might be potentially useful for practice, the following plan is suggested:

1. The selector of research methods should delineate his tasks and functions so that he can specify those aspects of his work that require information-processing techniques.
2. He determines the extent to which his particular practice functions correspond to a problem-solving model. He then locates that specific component of practice in which he believes

he needs to improve his information-processing procedures. For example, a social caseworker may not be satisfied with the information he gathers for making assessments of marital difficulties in couples seeking counseling.

3. He refers to Table 3 and selects the direct research analogue of practice. For example, the social caseworker interested in assessment would identify problem formulation as its research analogue. In addition, he should locate other research components which might be related to assessment or problem formulation. In general, research observational techniques and sampling methods may be employed in all components of practice; they are useful as information gathering techniques and as cost reducing procedures, respectively.

4. He locates information related to research methods used in the research analogues selected in item 3 above. Utilizing the research literature or seeking assistance through colleagues who are knowledgeable about research methods, he locates various techniques that have been employed in problem formulation, e.g., procedures for specifying concepts so they are amenable to observations and measurement. Moreover, since sampling procedures and data collection devices could be employed in problem formulation, he would attempt to locate such methods which could be used in practice. For example, the caseworker interested in assessing marital difficulties may locate methods for developing questionnaires, interviews and tests.

5. When the social worker is interested in specific concepts, such as marital satisfaction-dissatisfaction, the search can be more direct, i.e., he locates information that bears on the concept and on techniques that might have been used in research studies to explicate that concept. With respect to marital satisfaction-dissatisfaction, he may refer to literature on marriage and the family, or to available compilations of indicators of marital stability in research texts and manuals. For example, in Miller's *Handbook of Research Design and Social Measurement*, there is a section pertaining to family and marriage which includes marriage prediction and marital adjustment

schedules—instruments used as indicators of marital satisfaction and adjustment.[30]

6. If specific techniques are located, he reviews those procedures with respect to their potential use in practice. In this regard, the preceding sections on "dimensions affecting the use of social research methods" and "preconditions for using research methods" are pertinent.

7. If no direct techniques are available, he can consider the possibility of developing information-processing instruments based on principles for developing research observational techniques. In particular, social workers could use their knowledge of interviewing, in conjunction with principles of interview schedule and questionnaire construction to develop their own instruments in relation to their information processing needs.

The above plan is offered as a device for selecting research methods which could be useful for practice. Some aspects of practice may not fit the problem-solving model precisely. Moreover, there may not be, in some instances of practice, a direct analogue to the problem-solving model of research. This scheme is not offered as the only way to select research methods; it is presented so that social work practitioners and researchers can think about and be sensitized to the possible analogues in their work. It is a plan from which selectors of research methods can depart—formulating those models most appropriate to their particular concerns. Furthermore, the plan has been employed for developing and locating some suggested uses of research methods for social work practice.

Suggested Uses of Research Methods

ASSESSMENT

The component of practice in which research methods may be most helpful is assessment. Techniques that are useful for assessment in social casework are behavioral assessment instruments, personality inventories, projective tests, attitude scales, psychiatric rating scales, and principles for constructing and using questionnaires and interviews. Behavioral assessment instruments are used by proponents of behavior modification, and they can be located by referring to books on behavior modification and by reading publications such as the *Journal of Applied Behavioral Analysis*. Included in behavioral assessment instruments are means of obtaining frequencies of baseline behaviors and formulating questions pertaining to reinforcement schedules.[31] Many social caseworkers refer to assessments made by clinical psychologists on the basis of personality inventories and projective tests, and some caseworkers have used psychological tests themselves in certain aspects of their work. In essence, psychological tests are research methods employed for assessment purposes — the Minnesota Multiphasic Personality Inventory, the Draw-A-Person Test, the Thematic Apperception Test, etc.[32] Rating scales and attitude questionnaires may also be utilized for assessment. For example, the U.S. Public Health Service has a compendium of psychiatric rating scales, used for assessing social adjustment, moods, and behaviors of patients in psychiatric institutions.[33] The social caseworker who is interested in locating procedures for determining the attitudes of his clients in particular areas — such as punitiveness or permissiveness in child management — may turn to books and research articles which include attitude scales. For example, *Scales for the Measurement of Attitudes* contains a number of attitude scales related to such topics as social practices, social issues and problems, and social institutions.[34] Of possible interest to caseworkers in family service agencies are scales rating "attitudes toward family-related practices" and "attitudes toward members of the family." [35] Those scales may be used to assess a client's attitudes toward his family, and they may serve as indices of change. The caseworker interested in assessing the client's perception of himself in relation to other persons might refer to Kelly's personality theory; he would find the Role Construct Repertory Test, which has been used to assess problems in role relations and to register change in those relations as a function of treatment.[36]

Moreover, when no specific assessment instruments are available, the caseworker may form his own by referring to principles of questionnaire and interview construction which are widely available in textbooks on research methods.

The group worker may use any of the above assessment devices. In addition, he may employ instruments for assessing different aspects of group functioning—group interaction, group cohesiveness, and so forth. He could turn to the literature on group dynamics, which contains a variety of group assessment procedures, and to such periodicals as *Sociometry* and the *Journal of Personality and Social Psychology*. The community organizer, administrator, and social planner can use techniques from sample survey research to determine needs, resources, and the use of resources in a community. In particular, the selection of samples may make their assessment tasks more efficient, i.e., information may be obtained more quickly at lower costs. A great deal of experience has been accumulated in social research regarding questionnaire construction, interviewing, ways to reduce bias, etc. Hence, the social worker could consult with research methodologists and / or refer to such books as *Reducing the Cost of Surveys* and *Survey Design and Analysis*.[37] Moreover, research techniques pertaining to the construction of social indicators are essential for planning and for determining the progress made in nations, states, and communities. Of obvious concern and importance is the measurement of morbidity rates, mortality rates, literacy rates, economic income available to families, and the extent, type, and duration of crime, delinquency, mental illness, and so forth. The volume, *Toward a Social Report*, is addressed to the use of such indicators for describing the state of the nation in regard to social issues and problems, and for planning national goals.[38]

INTERVENTION

Research methods are potentially useful for the formulation of intervention plans—especially if they can be employed for articulating typologies of social work intervention related to assessment. Although such a need has long been recognized in social work, treatment typologies that are consistently applicable and effective are not available.[39] However, some research dealing with the problem of differential treatment has been conducted, and it may provide some useful ideas for practitioners. Hollis has devised a treatment typology, and she has related it to the case-worker's assessment of personality functioning; Palmer and Warren have conducted research on differential treatment for delinquents, based on the maturity levels of delinquents and those of parole agents; and Kernberg and his associates have developed hypotheses on differential treatment in psychoanalysis and psychotherapy, based on the client's ego strength and on the therapist's skill.[40] Contained in those reports are methods that can be used to classify treatment methodologies through interviews, rating devices, and content analyses. Since the level of knowledge regarding the effectiveness of differential treatment is low (i.e., at the levels of concepts and hypotheses), the practitioner ultimately resorts to the method of trial and error. Thus, research methods might be useful to delineate criteria for appraising the extent to which the social worker's implementation procedures appear to be appropriate. In this regard, the social work practitioner may develop brief questionnaires and / or questions to use in interviewing his clients, content analyses for reviewing the reactions of participants in interviews and meetings, and rating scales which could be employed to systematize judgments about the workability of intervention plans. For example, the social caseworker may use a system for analyzing the contents of interviews in order to specify his use of intervention techniques; [41] the group worker can appraise the nature of topics discussed in the group, and the usefulness of those topics as perceived by the group members; [42] the community organizer may maintain logs of intervention endeavors and classify those efforts in relation to the responses of his clientele. Such procedures may enable social workers to systematically record their experiences, hence enabling them to develop hypotheses about appropriate and inappropriate interventions in the context of their specific practice.

EVALUATION, TERMINATION, AND FOLLOW-UP

Many practice evaluations are made on the basis of reassessments over time; in essence, the extent and nature of the problem is evaluated to determine whether the problem is persistent, exacerbated, or ameliorated. Research methods are especially useful for such purposes, for they provide principles and techniques for making assessments, determining change, and inferring the relationship between change and intervention strategies. For example, a caseworker may have an objective of enhancing the self concept of his client. To determine whether there are changes in self concept, the caseworker would have to specify indicators of that dimension so that changes can be observed. He might employ self concept attitude scales, or form judgments of the client's self concept in his assessment. He would then have a reference point for observing possible changes in the client's self concept over time. Moreover, he may possibly adopt some principles of experimentation. For example, the client may be assigned to a waiting list because of the large caseloads in the agency. Determination of self concept at initial contact, at the beginning of intervention, and at subsequent points in intervention, may provide evidence of an association between intervention and changes in self concept, i.e., if there are no changes between initial contact and the end of the waiting period, but there are changes between the initiation of treatment and subsequent treatment stages.

Evaluations of progress contain information which relates to the goals of practice. To the extent that those goals can be translated into observable indicators, information related to goal achievements can be attained. In this regard, research methodology can help; not only in providing principles and techniques of observation, but also in specifying observable indicators. For example, *Social Program Evaluation* indicates how objectives of health, education, and welfare programs can be specified so that evaluative information can be provided with respect to goal achievement.[43] Indeed, that text was utilized for developing brief examples of evaluation in a previous section of this chapter, "information correspondence."

Information pertinent to termination and follow-up is provided by evaluations of progress over time. As indicated earlier, follow-up information can be obtained by such devices as interviewing by telephone, mailed questionnaires, and direct observations. Furthermore, information can be provided through the systematic compilation of agency statistics concerning agency expenditures, the provision of services, and agency referral patterns. Certainly, information pertinent to the accomplishment of practice goals is vital; especially with reference to the conduct of social work practice and with respect to the desire for maintaining social work accountability—to clientele, social workers, related professionals, sponsors of social agencies, and the public.

Chapter 5

~·~

Abusing Social
Research

In earlier chapters, the emphasis has been on the proper use of substantive and methodological knowledge. To further increase the student's potential for effectively using research, it is instructive to consider how research can be abused. One is more likely to use research knowledge appropriately if he can recognize possible abuses of that knowledge. As defined herein, abuses refer to unethical procedures and distortions in producing, communicating, receiving, and implementing social research. In essence, abuses are errors which detract from the fundamental purposes of social research—the production and communication of reliable knowledge. Moreover, abuses can occur, irrespective of the intent of the producer or user of knowledge. Unintentional errors made through negligence, carelessness, or ignorance are mild forms of abuse, whereas more serious abuses are those that are made when the abusers are aware of them. Thus, abuses can range from misapplications of appropriate levels of knowledge to the deliberate distortion or suppression of research data for personal and / or political ends.

The purpose of this chapter is not to identify abusers; rather, it is to consider a series of potential abuses that could render social research ineffective. These abuses have been abstracted from the literature and my own experiences in teaching, research, and consultation to social agencies. Such abuses will be presented as hypothetical ones, although similar abuses have been observed in research and social work practice.

As previously indicated, the transmission and reception of research knowledge involves the following: the initiation of social research, conducting research and communicating substantive and methodological results, accurately receiving those results, and implementing them in social work practice. Since abuses are inappropriate or ineffective uses, they can be located in each of the above areas pertinent to the process of communicating research results. The abuses to be presented are not exhaustive, but they provide a range of possibilities which should be sufficient for the purpose of sensitizing the student to the kinds of abuses that can take place.

Abuses in the Initiation
of Research

Typical situations included in the "initiation of research" are those in which social researchers are hired to conduct research on agency problems, or to evaluate the efficiency and effectiveness of social programs. Although there are abuses in the initiation of research not specifically geared to social work practice, those abuses are not of primary concern here, because there is less of a possibility for the social worker (as a consumer of research) to influence or to engage in those abuses. There are four major abuses that can occur in the initiation of research pertinent to social work: violations of agreements between researchers, sponsors, and administrators; administrative limitations on knowledge alternatives; research as posture; and research as management control.

VIOLATIONS OF AGREEMENTS

During the initiation stages of research, important relations are established between the sponsors of research, the administrators of social agencies, and social researchers. These relations include mutual obligations for the conduct and reporting of social research: the conditions under which the research is to be conducted; the purposes of the research; time limitations for completion of research; provisions for access to relevant information; and ethical considerations about potential harm to participants in the research—their informed consent, and issues of confidentiality and invasion of privacy. All of those preceding considerations could lead to abuses, particularly if the mutual obligations among researchers, sponsors, and other important parties are not spelled out at the onset. To the extent that obligations are understood and agreed upon, the likelihood of potential abuse is reduced considerably. Obviously, the violation of a contract or an agreement is an abuse. For example, an administrator of a correctional institution and a researcher studying the effectiveness of that agency may agree that the findings of the research should be reviewed by an advisory group associated with the institution, prior to the release of information for public consumption. The researcher may violate that agreement by releasing the information without subjecting his conclusions to review by the advisory group; correspondingly, the administrator may violate that agreement by not allowing the results to be released at all. In the same study, both the administrator and the researcher might have agreed that the findings would not be used to identify, reward, or punish staff persons who appear to facilitate or hinder organizational effectiveness. If the agreement is violated, it is an abuse of the rights of those persons who participated. In that instance the abuse is not a direct distortion of knowledge, but it is a misuse of knowledge in that it violates an ethical position agreed upon prior to the conduct of the research—without such assurances, the research subjects might not have provided accurate information about their contributions to organizational effectiveness (or ineffectiveness).

An example of an abuse related to the contractual obligations of the researcher and his sponsor is one in which the researcher agrees to seek one type of knowledge, but actually is interested in another. The sponsor may want information which could be employed for improving a social agency, while the researcher may not be interested in the effectiveness of the agency, but rather in some pet theories or ideas he wants to pursue. Such an abuse is often difficult to recognize because one can argue that abstract, theoretical studies ultimately can be related to many practical considerations. However, that kind of abuse is possible when the following conditions are present: the researcher needs funds to continue his own line of research, the research is conceived in relatively abstract and esoteric terminology, and the sponsor is not aware of the specific nature of the research.[1] In contrast, researchers can be deceived by sponsors. The extent to which the research is initiated and the findings are released may depend upon social and political pressures exerted on the sponsor, and the sponsor may not reveal that information to the researcher. Hippel and Primack have identified abuses which occur in the executive levels of government regarding the release of scientific information; and Lang has provided case studies which deal with the political control of research on civil disorder and educational achievement.[2] The essential point is that research information is abused when it is available (or unavailable according to its support or lack of support) for sociopolitical decisions, rather than being made available as a function of researcher-sponsor agreements. Hence a major set of abuses can occur when there is a failure to specify and to adhere to contractual obligations between researchers and their sponsors.

ADMINISTRATIVE LIMITATIONS ON RESEARCH ALTERNATIVES

A second type of abuse in the initiation of research is one in which the administrator of a social agency calls for a study for which he limits the alternatives. For example, an administrator of a social casework agency may be interested in the extent to which clients improve as a result of casework intervention, but not in other alternatives, i.e., the extent to which clients do not change or even get worse. In an evaluation of an agency, an administrator may be interested only in the efforts of his staff, rather than in their effectiveness and efficiency. A sponsor of delinquency research may believe that funds should be invested in the rehabilitation of delinquents in communities rather than in institutions. He may be more interested in institutional "failures" than in institutional "successes"; and he may limit those alternatives to a study of "failures" only.

An abuse is apparent when the alternatives are limited so that a program can only "look good" or "look bad." The researcher can participate in this abuse by emphasizing the search for information related to a possible desire of the sponsor—the seeking of information to support opinions he has already formulated. Certainly, a function of the researcher through preliminary discussions with the sponsor is to indicate the possible alternatives and to point out the kinds of knowledge that could result by either expanding or limiting the alternatives for study.

For example, the following statement may appear to make a casework agency "look good": "Eighty percent of the persons receiving casework help have improved." With the presentation of additional information, the agency may not look as good. The persons who received help may have been comprised of only those clients who have completed more than five interviews. That is, 40 out of 50 persons (80 percent) who had more than five interviews may have been rated as improved by social caseworkers. In addition, of 400 persons who received less than five interviews, 40 (10 percent) may have been judged to have shown improvement. Moreover, other casework agencies with similar clientele may have shown 70 percent improvement for all clients. Thus, the limiting of alternatives for study can lead to distortions in information produced by social research.

RESEARCH AS POSTURE

A third type of abuse in the initiation of research occurs when an administrator calls for research for the purpose of "posture," but not for the objective of producing knowledge. Posture is the image of the agency which the administrator wishes to convey to the public. The mildest form of this abuse is when an agency sponsors small-scale research for the purpose of providing an image of "objectivity, accountability, and innovation." The administrator may regard research as "a good thing"; but he does not pay attention to the kind of research that is done, nor to the relationship of research knowledge to social work practice. Research studies are conducted, and research reports are filed away and ignored. Yet, in public relations encounters, the image of objectivity is fostered—simply because the agency has research activities in operation.

A more serious form of abuse may arise when conflict occurs, and the initiation of research is used as a political strategy in an attempt to minimize the conflict. For example, a group of citizens in an urban community (influenced by community organizers) may protest to the city manager about the parking meters newly installed in their neighborhood, and the large number of parking violations they have been charged with. Furthermore, there are no parking meters in other residential neighborhoods of the community.[3] The citizens may demand that the parking meters be removed, while the officials in "city hall" want to delay action.

The city manager and his staff call for a study to look at parking meter violations in the neighborhood and throughout the city in order to learn about the attitudes of other residents who may not be represented by the group of protesters; to map out the areas of the city with parking meters; and so forth. If no information about parking meters and parking meter violations is available, research could be used effectively to provide data for decision-making at the city governmental level. However, if the information is available and if additional information is conjured as necessary for decision-making, the call for research is a device for delay. The purpose of the tactic of delay is to persuade the protesters that additional information is required before new decisions can be made. The posture is one of willingness to respond, but only after more extensive information is gathered which bears on the issue—information which was not needed when previous decisions had been made regarding the installation of parking meters.

Thus, research can be abused by being considered as a device to placate a group of protesters and to delay action. The abuse is clear, for example, when the protesting group drops its demands, and the research efforts of city hall are also discontinued. If the research is completed, it is more difficult to determine whether the abuse of research as posture is maintained. An abuse may take place if the results of the research are not released, or if it can be demonstrated that the knowledge produced by the research was already available.

The abuse of posture is also possible in national commissions which have been created to investigate such social issues as the impact of television on violence, and the reasons for riots and other civil disorders in the United States.[4] Lang's concluding remarks about the Kerner Commission's use of social scientists (as researchers) are pertinent:

> If the use made by the Kerner Commission of its social science input is any guide at all, we may conclude that members of such commissions are likely to be bound by and to present quantitative data that, used in a report, give it the aura of objectivity. But when issues arise over how to interpret such data, the social scientist becomes involved in delicate negotiations in which he finds it hard to separate his professional role from his role as a member of the commission, involved in its internal politics.[5]

RESEARCH AS MANAGEMENT CONTROL

A fourth type of abuse in the initiation of social research is that of using research as management control. This refers to an administrator's use of research as a tactic to control his staff; it does not refer to the commonly accepted notion of employing the techniques of research to provide data as a "management tool" for making rational decisions.[6] For example, the professional staff of an organization which has the purpose of fostering equal opportunities for all of the residents in a local community may be comprised of several community organizers. The community organizers may use different approaches, or they may employ strategies that are antithetical to those of the director of the organization. The director would like his staff to use a uniform approach that is more consistent with his views, but he is not able to persuade his staff that uniformity is necessary. The director hires a researcher to evaluate his program; the researcher is experimentally oriented and indicates that the program procedures should be standardized (i.e., made more uniform) before the program can be evaluated. But this stipulation is then used by the administrator as an opportunity to force the staff into standardized procedures; for he believes the staff may be somewhat fearful of the evaluation since it might indicate that the program is not as effective as it could be.

The administrator's purpose is to use the evaluation, which has the ostensive objective of providing information to improve the program, as a strategy to obtain staff compliance. If the results of the evaluation are ignored by the director, it is an abuse of social research. Obviously, the only persons who would know the extent of the abuse are the administrator and, possibly, the researcher. It is abusive in that the intent is to threaten the community organizers to comply with administrative desire by deceiving them about the purposes of the evaluation.

It is not intended to imply that abuses occur most of the time, or that administrators and researchers are typically partners in a collusive process whereby research is invidiously employed for purposes other than that of seeking knowledge. Instead, the objective is merely to point out the kinds of abuses that might occur when research is initiated in social agencies. To the extent that those possible abuses are recognized, research is more likely to be used effectively.

Abuses in the Conduct and Communication of Research

Most social workers are not involved in the initiation of social research. They often rely on research communications, without being aware of how the research studies were conducted. To accurately receive such communications, it is helpful to have some notions about the possible abuses that could take place in the conduct of social research and in the communication of methodological and substantive knowledge. Four interrelated areas have been selected, within which a number of potential abuses can be presented: ethical abuses, omissions of information, faulty conclusions, and statistical abuses.

ETHICAL ABUSES

Ethical abuses involve the inflicting of potential harm on subjects who participate in research, and / or the reporting of data which violates the rights of research participants. Although not directly related to social work, an example of a serious ethical abuse is that of an experimental study conducted by the U.S. Public Health Service. The research was initiated in 1932, and it had the purpose of following up 425 poor, black persons with latent syphilis and 200 poor, black persons who did not have syphilis, in order to study the course of syphilis over time. At the beginning of the study there was no cure for syphilis, but after fifteen years penicillin was found (in other studies) to be an effective remedy. In spite of that, the study continued for twenty-five more years; and the Public Health Service did not provide the subjects with penicillin unless they asked for it. The abuse was that of not providing a known, effective treatment when it was available and, according to *Time* Magazine:

> Such a failure seems almost beyond belief, or human compassion. Recent reviews of 125 cases by the PHS's Center for Disease Control in Atlanta found that half had syphilitic heart valve damage. Twenty-eight had died of cardiovascular or central nervous system problems that were complications of syphilis.[7]

A similar issue pertinent to social work is that of the use of control groups. For example, a particular mode of psychotherapy may be provided for clients in an experimental group, but not for clients in a control group. Whether or not the use of control groups is abusive depends upon the state of knowledge that exists at the time of the experiment. If it is unknown whether the psychotherapy is effective or ineffective, then it is no more abusive to deny treatment than it is to give it. In contrast, if an effective means of treatment is available, subjects should have access to it; or if an effective treatment is discovered while the research is in progress, as in the example of the study on syphilis, the research should be discontinued.

Another type of ethical abuse is that of releasing information which clearly identifies individual research participants, without having their approval. This is a violation of a researcher's ethical obligations to his research subjects. For example, a study of a "multi-problem family" which indicates its experiences and frustrations with legal, welfare, employment, and medical agencies may be extremely embarrassing and potentially harmful to the family.

The release of information is potentially harmful if it adversely affects the lives of the research subjects. A survey of housing needs may include questions regarding dissatisfactions of respondents in their current living situation. Suppose the research subjects live in a housing project, and they are identified in the research report. The housing officials may respond in a vindictive manner toward those persons, e.g., not attending to needed housing repairs, ignoring complaints, etc.

A related type of abuse is the reporting of research results (in which the respondents have not been identified) that have been obtained by unethical means. For example, a laboratory experiment may be conducted on the extent to which persons are willing to harm other persons. In the conduct of the experiment, the subjects are intentionally deceived, i.e., a confederate of the experimenter deliberately provokes the respondents so that the experimenter can determine what kinds of provocation lead to aggressive statments and/or actions toward the confederate. After the experiment is concluded, the researcher may explain the deception to his respondents, but they may not give their consent to release the results. If the results are released by the researcher, he is abusing the respondents' rights of informed consent, which is the right to participate (or not participate) after the subjects know what the research is about.

There are essentially four basic ethical issues which must be rigorously adhered to by researchers in the pursuit of knowledge when using human subjects. These are informed consent, the invasion of privacy, confidentiality, and physical and mental harm. Indeed, these issues have warranted sufficient attention so that sponsoring bodies of research, such as the National Institute of Mental Health, have demanded reviews of research proposals by committees comprised of the investigators' peers. Those committees determine the extent to which research should be conducted, with due consideration to ethical principles involving the rights of human subjects: the voluntary nature of participation, low risks of personal harm, and the freedom from invasion of privacy. These issues are regarded as important in our society, and they are the subject of much discussion among professional researchers.[8] The essential point is that the bulk of social research knowledge comes from human research subjects, and abuses of social research may occur when their rights are violated.

OMISSIONS OF INFORMATION

Abuses of social research may take place when researchers fail to include sufficient detail about their research procedures. The receiver of research communications should have enough information to determine whether research conclusions are appropriately based on the data gathered in research studies.[9] Of course, the amount of detail depends upon the vehicle of communication used by the researcher, i.e., article, monograph, book, or oral report. Some professional journals, for example, may limit the amount of methodological information to be reported. Nevertheless, information about the procedures of research—either in the body of a report, or in other references indicated to the receiver of research communications—should be available so that the level of resultant knowledge can be appraised. Otherwise, if only the conclusions are communicated, the receiver of the communication must rely on his faith in the reputation of the communicator, or in the status of the communication source. Such a situation could lead to research abuses.

For example, suppose that an "expert" has conducted a study of citizens' participation groups. He believes those groups are desirable for obtaining changes in social policy. Although many persons might agree with that value, an abuse could occur if he reports that citizen participation has led to more effective decision-making, without indicating the data from which his conclusions were derived. He might, in fact, have no data, or data that lead to equivocal conclusions. Both expert and novice have the responsibility to present data on which conclusions are based— conclusions which may be supportive of, or in opposition to, the researcher's basic values.

An example of an omission of information about research procedures was reported by Cain.[10] He indicated that a research study, which produced a profile of the aged population in the United States, claimed that the elderly did not have major social and health needs. However, the researchers did not clearly communicate the fact that their study was based on a sample of the elderly heavily weighted toward the upper and middle economic classes, and which excluded all non-whites, all persons living in public housing, and all persons receiving old age assistance. The sample was not representative of that aged population that is likely to require health and medical services, and which is less able to afford them. Hence, important information was omitted in the researcher's presentation. If that distortion had not been located, serious implications regarding social policy for the aged might have ensued. The study was sponsored by the American Medical Association, which was not in favor of liberalized health plans for the aged. Moreover, it appeared as if the study was being used for political purposes.

FAULTY CONCLUSIONS

Researchers should exercize proper caution in interpreting their data, and in presenting their research findings. Failure to do so could result in faulty or erroneous conclusions, which are abuses of social research. Four types of faulty conclusions are presented: conclusions based on nonrepresentative samples; conclusions based on inadequate controls; conclusions based on unreliable and invalid data; and conclusions based on inappropriate assumptions about research data.

Conclusions Based on Nonrepresentative Samples

In the conduct of social research, the researcher identifies the target population to which he wishes to generalize, and he often employs sampling procedures to obtain representative samples so that he can make inferences about that population. The researcher's conclusions must be evaluated by the sample that he uses. Faulty conclusions could be made by simply ignoring the sample and assuming that it is identical to the target population. As indicated above, a profile of the aged population is inaccurate if it is based on a sample not representative of that population. It is important to note that a distortion could take place even if the research procedures are included in the research report. The researcher may not emphasize the disparity between the sample and the population, and the receiver of his research communications may overlook the possibility of faulty conclusions.

For example, a study may be conducted to describe characteristics of teenagers who are drug addicts—characteristics such as performance in school, family economic circumstances, and types of drugs used. The target population may be comprised of teenage drug addicts in an urban community. Suppose the researcher obtains his sample of addicts from a list of families receiving money from the welfare department. Obviously, the sample (and the population) is restricted to families which would be regarded as lower class. The researcher conducts his survey, and he finds that 2 percent of the teenagers in 200 families are addicted to heroin, and all of those heroin addicts have been adjudicated as delinquents by the courts. The description of those teenagers is, at best, representative of those whose families are receiving welfare. The sample is not representative of teenagers from higher income families. If the researcher generalizes from his study of all teenagers in the community, he is making conclusions on the basis of a nonrepresentative sample—and those conclusions may be inaccurate and misleading. In essence, the researcher may make an erroneous conclusion, but not be aware of it. This is a different type of abuse than one in which the researcher, or his sponsor, deliberately misleads by suppressing or omitting relevant information.

Another example of improper generalizations could be in a study testing the hypothesis that continuance (defined as more than five completed interviews between a caseworker and his client) is correlated with the extent to which the client and the caseworker have similar perceptions of the clients' problems and needs. Suppose the study is conducted in a correctional agency, where it is mandatory for the clients to keep appointments. In that instance, there should be no relationship between the perception of clients' problems and needs, and continuance, because clients are essentially coerced into having contacts with caseworkers. If the researcher generalizes that zero-order relationship to all social workers and to all social agencies, he is clearly in error. In contrast, suppose that a study is conducted in a mental health clinic for voluntary clients. It may be found that clients continue to make contacts with their caseworkers when the caseworkers define clients' problems in the same way that clients do. In addition, when there is a disparity between the perceptions of the caseworkers and the clients, clients discontinue making contacts with the caseworkers. Thus, there is a relationship between continuance and client-caseworker perceptions. That finding could not be accurately generalized to the correctional agency which requires regular contacts, e.g., a probation department, a prison, a bureau of paroles.

Conclusions Based on Inadequate Control

Conclusions about the testing of cause-effect hypotheses should be made with respect to the degree of internal control that is provided in research studies. When there is a low degree of internal control or the control procedures are inadequate, conclusions about causality should be appropriately qualified. If such qualifications are not considered, the conclusions may be erroneous.

Suppose that an experiment was conducted to test the hypothesis that guided group interaction (a technique employed in

group counseling) for junior high-school boys who have difficulties in school will lead to increases in attendance and school performance. Half of the boys with behavioral problems in one junior high school were assigned to an experimental group which
received guided group interaction, while the remaining boys
were assigned to a control group which did not receive guided
group interaction. Procedures such as randomization, matching,
and statistical control were not employed. After six months of
guided group interaction, the experimental and control groups
were compared on school attendance and on grades. It was reported that the group of boys who received guided group interaction had a "C" average and attended 80 percent of its classes,
while the control group had a "D" average and attended 70 percent of its classes. The conclusion was made that guided group
interaction is a causal factor which leads to desirable changes in
school performance.

That conclusion may be erroneous, particularly if the two
groups of boys were not equivalent with respect to the variables
of grades and attendance prior to the introduction of guided
group interaction, i.e., the experimental group may have been
chosen because of its earlier, superior performance in school.
Moreover, it may be found, for example, that at the beginning of
the experiment, the experimental and the control groups exhibited the same differences in performance as they did after six
months of guided group interaction. Therefore, the appropriate
conclusion would be that there were no changes in grades and
school attendance for either the experimental or the control
group, and that guided group interaction does not appear to be
causally related to increased school performance.

One can locate other errors by determining the extent to which
researchers fail to qualify their conclusions with respect to the
control procedures that are necessary for determining causality.
In this regard, the reader can refer to chapter 2, where discussions of internal control and evidence for testing causal hypotheses are presented. These types of abuses are essentially inappropriate conclusions that are based on ineffective uses of control
procedures in experimental and quasi-experimental studies.

Conclusions Based on Unreliable and Invalid Data

The results of empirical research investigations for testing hypotheses—descriptive, correlational, or cause-effect—are dependent upon the accuracy of the measurements employed. Researchers should consider the extent to which data are reliable and valid, and they should attempt to minimize bias in the collection of data. Abuses could occur if conclusions are made without regard to the dependability of the data collected. For example, a social planner may be interested in the degree to which working mothers would use day care centers. A survey of working mothers is conducted, and they are asked whether they currently use day care centers. A low proportion of working mothers respond that they do, and it might be concluded that additional day care centers are not necessary. The conclusions may be erroneous because the data may not be valid. The working mothers' current uses of day care centers may be minimal because few day care centers are available. Moreover, those mothers might utilize such centers if they are convenient, more economical than hiring baby sitters, and furnish more enjoyable environments for their children. Thus, the failure to obtain more information regarding the need for day care centers and their potential utilization could lead to false conclusions.

Another example of a potential abuse could be a study which seeks to describe the relationship between delinquency and the degree of parental supervision for adolescent boys. Suppose all of the data are collected by questionnaires completed by boys in junior and senior high schools. The questions deal with whether the boys indicate that they have committed offenses which could be regarded as delinquent, and with such topics as whether their parents have rules for supervision and enforce those rules. Conclusions made about parental supervision and its effects on delinquency could be erroneous because of unreliable and invalid data. The boys may either under- or over-report the extent of their delinquency, i.e., perceived delinquency may not be related to adjudicated delinquency. Furthermore, the boys' perceptions of parental supervision may be distorted and not representative of the *actual* behaviors of parents.

Still another example of a potential abuse may be observed in a study that attempts to describe the aggressive behavior of casework clients on the basis of case records. Suppose that several judges read the records, and then make ratings on the degree of aggressivity in clients. Conclusions based on such data may be erroneous for the following reasons: 1) Caseworkers who compiled the records may not have had similar conceptions of aggressive behavior; 2) The recordings may have been based only on information obtained in casework interviews, and the interviews may not be representative of the clients' aggressive behaviors in their daily lives; 3) The caseworkers may have written their records from one to two months after the interviews were completed, thus allowing for the possibility of perceptual distortion; 4) Caseworkers may have varied with respect to the information they recorded about aggressive behavior. The recordings may not have been made for the explicit purpose of describing such behavior, thus, there may be incomplete information in a number of cases; 5) The judges' criteria for aggressive behavior may be different from those of the caseworkers. Moreover, the judges may not agree among themselves.

When a researcher presents his conclusions in the context of the limitations of his data, he is appropriately using social research. In contrast, the researcher who presents conclusions without communicating the limitations of his data is abusing social research by communicating inaccurate results, which could be misleading to those who wish to apply social research knowledge.

Conclusions Based on Inappropriate Assumptions about Research Data

Conclusions based on inappropriate assumptions about research data refer to logical errors in data interpretations. Perhaps the most serious error is that of assuming that the mere collection of data, whether or not it is relevant to the objectives of research, is sufficient for making conclusions. In other words, a researcher may make conclusions on the basis of data not pertinent to the phenomenon under study. Suppose that a certain research objective is to compare the effectiveness of individual as opposed to group supervision. A case study may have been conducted in which data were obtained about the procedures used in individual and group supervision: the number of meetings, the topics of discussion, etc. The researcher may not have gathered information about the effectiveness of supervision, such as increased knowledge and skills among the supervisees. Nevertheless, because data were collected about the efforts that took place in supervision, the researcher might assume that those data can also be used to make conclusions about effectiveness.

Another example is that of a study concerned with the degree of neighborhood participation in a community organization program. The researcher may conclude that program participants are in favor of the ideology espoused by the community organizers, in spite of the fact that no data regarding "ideology" were collected. The error is that the researcher assumes that program participants (who may have participated for a variety of reasons, none of which necessarily relate to the community organizers' ideologies) share the ideological positions of the organizers, simply because of their participation. The conclusion is premature, and it is erroneous until it is substantiated by empirical data.

Hirschi and Selvin have discussed a number of errors that researchers make in interpreting data, and several examples derived from their work should be sufficient to give the reader an idea of the kinds of faulty conclusions that can occur by misinterpreting relevant data. In particular, they have identified fallacies such as the following: the "profile fallacy," the "ecological fallacy," and the "syllogistic fallacy." [11]

The profile fallacy takes place when one summarizes a set of data descriptive of a group of persons to describe the average or typical person. For example, data may have been gathered about the characteristics of 100 clients who seek casework help. The group of clients has an average age of 30 years, 60 percent are married; 70 percent are female; 55 percent rent houses; and 75 percent are white. The error is to conclude that the average client (who does not exist) is a composite of the averages of all of the characteristics; i.e., the typical client is *a* young, white, female, married adult who lives in a rented house. The problem is that the above group traits cannot be logically added together to form a description of the average client. This is illustrated in Table 4 where it is observed that—contrary to the above profile—the majority of female clients do not live in rented houses. Although 70 percent of the clients are female and 55 percent rent houses, only 25 out of 70 females live in rented houses.

Table 4

Numbers of Male and Female Clients
Who Live in Rented Houses

	Living in Rented Houses	Not Living in Rented Houses	Totals
Female	25	45	70
Male	30	0	30
Totals	55	45	100

The "ecological fallacy" occurs when one assumes that a correlation referring to the properties of groups is synonymous with a correlation relating to the properties of individuals. For example, the proportion of minority persons and the prevalence of mental illness in the various census tracts of a community are variables based on group properties. Suppose there is a correlation between the two variables, i.e., those census tracts in the community which have lower proportions of minority persons also have lower rates of mental illness. One is in error if he infers from that "ecological correlation" that minority persons are more likely to become mentally ill than are nonminority persons. Before that conclusion could be made, more detailed analyses would have to be conducted; that is, correlations need to be computed with respect to the existence of mental illness for minority and nonminority persons *within* census tracts.[12]

The "syllogistic fallacy" takes place when one assumes that two variables, x and y, are strongly correlated if each is correlated to a third variable, z. Such an assumption is tenable when there is a perfect relationship ($r = 1.00$) between x and z, and between

y and z, but most of the relationships obtained in social research are at much lower levels of magnitude. Suppose that the correlation between social class (x) and psychosis (z) is $-.30$ (the lower the social class, the higher is the incidence of psychosis), while the correlation between self concept and psychosis is $-.40$ (the lower the self concept, the higher is the incidence of psychosis). It would be erroneous, without examining the joint relationships among x, y, and z to conclude that lower-class persons have lower self concepts and a greater susceptibility to mental illness than do persons in the higher social classes. Conclusions about the joint relationships among x, y, and z should be made only after such techniques as partial and multiple correlations are employed in the data analyses.[13]

STATISTICAL ABUSES *

Statistical abuses are errors in the application of statistical methods for analyzing and interpreting research data.[14] One common misuse of statistical methods is the employment of statistical tests of inference when the research sample is identical to the target population. Statistical tests are used to make inferences about statistical hypotheses, from a sample to a population from which the sample was derived. For example, one may infer that the hypothesis of a correlation being equivalent to zero should be rejected because the magnitude of the correlation in relation to the size of the sample could occur on a chance basis in only 5 out of 100 samples, i.e., the correlation is significant at or beyond the .05 level of probability.[15] In statistical inference, it is assumed that a number of possible samples could be obtained from a target population so that probability theory can be used to interpret such statistics as t, F, and chi square.[16]

* This section is optional reading for students who do not have an elementary understanding of statistical reasoning as described in introductory textbooks such as *Statistics in Social Research: An Introduction* by Robert S. Weiss (New York, Wiley, 1972). Although this brief section is addressed primarily to statistical problems in the production of research, it is to be noted that consumers of research can increase their skills in understanding and evaluating research knowledge by considering some of the potential abuses that can take place when producers of research inappropriately employ statistical methods.

However, when the total population is identical with the research sample, probability estimates are meaningless because
there is only one possible sample. In that case, the use of statistical inference is unnecessary, cumbersome, and potentially misleading. This is because it leads to confusion about the researcher's conception of the population; and the descriptions of the
sample are presented in a context which implies that there is less
certainty in the results than there actually is. When the target
population (and the sample) is defined as being comprised of 40
caseworkers in a public assistance agency, descriptive statistics
(such as percentages, means, and standard deviations) are sufficient for describing that population.[17] If the average case load
size is 50, it *is* 50. This is a different statement than one which is
based on statistical inference, e.g., the average case load size is
50, and it is statistically significant at or beyond the .05 probability level. The problem is that the researcher may erroneously
regard the probability statement as *ipso facto* more "scientific,"
while the receiver of his communication may regard it as "myth"
based on an appeal to the magic of probability theory.

A second statistical abuse occurs when a researcher hunts for
relationships in his data by using statistical tests; and after he
finds some statistically significant associations, he reports his
results as if they were based on *a priori* rather than *a posteriori*
hypotheses.[18] Suppose that a survey was conducted for seeking
correlates of client satisfaction in casework treatment. Client satisfaction was conceived as the dependent variable, and data
were collected on a large number of potentially independent
variables such as age, sex, education, and social class. No *a priori*
hypotheses about the relationships among those independent
variables and the dependent variable were formulated. Correlations might have been computed for each independent variable
and the dependent variable; and out of 100 correlations, two
were found to be statistically significant ($p < .05$). Those findings
should be reported in the following manner. The purpose was to
seek correlates of satisfaction; and out of 100 variables, two were
correlated with the dependent variable (employing the criterion
of statistical significance at the .05 level). The conclusion is that

the two correlations provide two hypotheses which can be tested in subsequent research. A misuse of statistical inference takes place if the researcher reports that the purpose of his study was to test two hypotheses, and the hypotheses were verified since statistically significant correlations were produced. Hence, the results of the study would be presented as evidence supporting a higher level of knowledge than the data indicate. Moreover, the "statistically significant" results may have been random events; that is, employing a .05 level of significance, 5 out of 100 correlations may be statistically significant on the basis of chance. Thus, in the above example, the two "statistically significant" associations could have occurred by chance. If the researcher fails to report that only 2 of the 100 possible correlations were statistically significant, he has distorted the meaning of statistical significance since he has not presented the complete context in which the statistical tests were performed.

A third statistical abuse takes place if the researcher substitutes a "one-tailed" test for a "two-tailed" test *after* he finds non-statistically significant results by using a two-tailed test of significance. A two-tailed test of significance is employed when the researcher makes a prediction of differences, but not of the direction of the differences. For example, an investigation may be concerned with comparing the effectiveness of group work versus social casework for juvenile delinquents in terms of recidivism. The researcher may expect differences in recidivism between those who receive casework or group work services, but he may not have any basis for predicting that either casework or group work will lead to more or less recidivism. Hence, the researcher uses a two-tailed test (e.g., on the differences between proportions of those who recidivate as a function of casework or group work), which is based on the technical notion that both ends (tails) of a sampling distribution (i.e., differences between proportions which show less recidivism for casework at one end, and differences between proportions which show less recidivism for group work at the other end) should be employed for making probability estimates.[19] In contrast, the researcher could employ a one-tailed test if he makes a prediction based on theo-

retical notions which specify, for example, that group work results in less recidivism than does social casework. In essence, he
would use only one end of a sampling distribution for making his
probability estimates.

At a given level of statistical significance, say at the .05 level, a
one-tailed test requires a lower magnitude of actual differences
between proportions than does a two-tailed test. For example, a
t-test for the differences between proportions of two groups comprised of 122 research subjects requires a magnitude of 1.980 or
higher to be statistically significant at the .05 level with a two-
tailed test, while a magnitude of 1.658 or higher is necessary for
statistical significance at the same level with a one-tailed test.[20]
The t-test is based on the magnitudes of the differences between
proportions, the sample sizes, and the variations from the average proportions in each of the two groups.[21]

A statistical abuse is illustrated in the following example. Suppose that the .05 level of significance is employed as the criterion
of statistical significance. The researcher finds that with a two-
tailed test, the differences between proportions are not statistically significant. He then switches to a one-tailed test and obtains a statistically significant value, which is the result that he
reports. In that instance, a criterion for testing the hypothesis
was changed (two-tailed to one-tailed test), and it is an abuse of
social research because more is made out of the data than is actually warranted.

A fourth abuse arises when one equates statistical significance
with practical significance.[22] Statistical significance depends
considerably on the size of the sample that is used to make inferences to a population. The larger the sample size, the smaller is
the difference between proportions that is required for statistical
significance. A difference between proportions of 10 percent for
a sample size of 200 is not statistically significant on a two-tailed
test at the .05 level, but the same difference between proportions
is statistically significant for a sample size of 2,000.

Practical significance depends on the nature and seriousness
of the problem being investigated, and it is not necessarily
equivalent to statistical significance. There may be a relationship

between the incidence of deteriorated housing conditions and lead poisoning in children, but it may not be statistically significant because of the small number of cases contained in the sample. The finding is practically significant because of the potential health hazards for children, and it should not be ignored because statistical significance has not been obtained. In contrast, a researcher may claim that his statistically significant results, secured from very large sample sizes, are practically significant. Suppose that the difference between the proportions of success for group work and casework is less than 1 percent, but statistically significant because of a large sample size. If the researcher accentuates the finding of statistical significance and deemphasizes the small percentage differences between the results of casework and group work, he could mislead the receivers of his research communications into believing that the relative effectiveness of group work is much greater than it actually is.

A fifth statistical abuse can take place by making misleading statements about percentages and frequencies.[23] If a researcher reports percentages and the numbers on which they are based, his interpretations can be checked against the data that are presented. However, results that are given solely in either numbers or percentages may be misleading. One might report that *only* 10 clients were dissatisfied with group work services in a particular agency. To be sure, 10 is a relatively small number; but if it is 10 out of 10 queried, that would represent *100 percent dissatisfaction*. Contrariwise, one might present the results only in terms of percentages. The statement, "80 percent of the clients are satisfied with group work services" could be misleading. Perhaps only 10 clients were interviewed, and all of those clients may have been keeping regular appointments with the agency for a long period of time. The satisfaction may not be as evident in a much larger number of clients who have received shorter-term services from the agency.

Although there are other abuses that take place in the application of statistical methods in social research, it is believed that the preceding five abuses are sufficient to sensitize the reader to the kinds of distortions that could result from inappropriate uses of statistical methods. For a more detailed analysis, the reader is referred to Wallis and Roberts' *The Nature of Statistics*, which indicates a number of other examples of statistical misuse.[24]

Abuses in Receiving Research Communications

Social work practitioners can abuse social research knowledge by failing to properly receive communications from social researchers. Distortions can take place in reading research literature, listening to oral reports of researchers, and in formal and informal conversations at conferences, meetings, and workshops. It is assumed that if the findings of social research are misinterpreted, it is probable that the applications of those results will be inappropriate. In this section, then, five sources of abuses in receiving social research knowledge are identified and discussed: 1) making inappropriate assumptions about levels of knowledge; 2) employing a framework of absolute certainty; 3) assuming all data are equally reliable and valid; 4) assuming that the same variable is defined identically in different studies; 5) employing false criteria of causality.

MAKING INAPPROPRIATE ASSUMPTIONS
ABOUT LEVELS OF KNOWLEDGE

Social workers make inappropriate assumptions about levels of knowledge when they regard the results of social research as being at either higher or lower levels of knowledge than is warranted. This abuse can occur when the social worker fails to assess the level of knowledge produced by the research. For example, a research study may have been conducted for the purpose of developing hypotheses that pertain to residential treatment for emotionally disturbed boys. The researcher may have been a participant observer, noting that those boys who are lower in the power structure of their peers at the treatment center are less likely to respond to individual treatment than boys who have more power (i.e., influence and control). The researcher may have concluded his study with the hypothesis that casework treatment goals will be enhanced if boys who have little influ-ence over their peers (and who are "scapegoated" by other boys) are assigned to special living units. An obvious abuse is for the receiver of that knowledge to regard it as a verified hypothesis by planning "special living arrangements" for boys who appear to have less "power" among their peers. The fact is that there is not sufficient information upon which to base that kind of decision. Moreover, it is possible that a special living arrangement may be more harmful than helpful. Without an evaluation of the con-sequences of assigning "low-power" boys to a special living unit, the decision to shift an institution's policy about living arrange-ments is premature.

In contrast, a social worker may assume that the level of re-search knowledge is lower than it really is. Suppose that a large number of research studies were designed to test hypotheses about the relative effectiveness of short-term as opposed to long-term social work intervention. Further, suppose that as a result of those studies, the data are consistent in favoring short-term treat-ment (e.g., three months or less) over long-term treatment. The implication is that social workers should consider whether shorter durations of intervention would be desirable at the social agencies in which they work. If the results of those studies are treated as hypotheses (rather than as partially verified or verified hypotheses), social work practitioners may not pay any attention at all to that kind of knowledge. Thus, assuming that the knowl-edge level is lower than it actually is could result in an error of omission.

EMPLOYING A FRAMEWORK OF ABSOLUTE CERTAINTY

A second type of abuse in receiving research communications occurs when the receiver indicates that he can only attend to research findings about which he is absolutely certain. This stance would lead to the rejection of most research knowledge. Moreover, if the social worker is consistent in employing the framework of absolute certainty, he would be forced to reject most knowledge about the practice of social work. Social re-searchers and social work practitioners do not have the "ultimate truth" at their finger tips; they try to approximate the truth in acquiring and using knowledge that may assist them in their work. But, employing a framework of absolute certainty can have more immediate import than philosophical discussions about the nature of truth.

Suppose, for example, a survey of AFDC recipients who live in a cold climate reveals that 25 percent of the 800 families interviewed have insufficient clothing and heating facilities for the winter months. The estimate of 25 percent may be in error by a few percentage points, and the researcher may indicate that it is possible that some of the families could have either over- or understated their needs. In essence, the researcher is not absolutely certain of the proportion of 25 percent need; nevertheless, it may be the best estimate available. A welfare administrator may refuse to act unless he knows *exactly* the extent of the problem—he wants a guarantee of absolute certainty before he makes a decision based on research results. Of course, the administrator could act by making sure that all of the AFDC families are prepared for the winter months. Although the example may be somewhat exaggerated, it illustrates the point that an expectancy of absolute certainty could lead to inertia when action is required.

A related abuse takes place when one rejects completely some, but not all, levels of knowledge. For example, one might indicate that the only levels of knowledge that should be accepted from research are empirical generalizations based on verified correlational and/or verified cause-effect hypotheses. This stance assumes that social work practitioners cannot use knowledge based on concepts, hypotheses, and verified descriptive hypotheses, i.e., ideas and simple facts. Such a position is abusive because it would lead to the failure to use information processing techniques in social work practice, research methods for acquiring approximations to knowledge, and a number of concepts and ideas which could aid social workers in their work.

ASSUMING ALL DATA ARE EQUALLY RELIABLE AND VALID

Assuming that all data are equally reliable and valid is an abuse that occurs when a receiver of research communications about two or more studies assumes that the data from those studies are necessarily equivalent. That is, data collected on the same phenomenon—irrespective of their degrees of accuracy— are combined to make generalizations about that phenomenon.

Suppose two different research studies are conducted in order to describe the extent to which low-income persons participate in community organizations. One study, A, is based on data gathered from a questionnaire distributed to a sample of low-income persons in a certain community. Included in the questionnaire are a series of questions about the respondents' socioeconomic characteristics, and only one question about participation in community organizations: "Are you currently participating in any community organizations and activities?" The other study, B, is based on data gathered from several sources: interviews with samples of low-income persons in several communities; interviews with representatives of community organizations in those communities; and examinations of available attendance and participation records of the community organizations in which the respondents said they participated. The low-income respondents are queried about what organizations they have participated in; whether they participate regularly; whether they want to increase or decrease participation, and the reasons for doing so; and their knowledge of existing organizations, and their perceptions of the purposes of those organizations. In addition, representatives of the community organizations are asked about the purposes of their organizations and the extent of participation among low-income persons. Moreover, data on actual participation as determined from the attendance records are used to validate the professed participation of the respondents.

The second study would have more reliable and valid data than the first study. An abuse would occur if the receiver of research communications regards the data from the two studies as equivalent. Suppose that study A indicates there is a high degree of participation, while study B indicates there is a low degree of participation. One might simply conclude that two studies on participation were conducted; one showed high participation, and one showed low participation. However, that conclusion is misleading because the data in A and B are not equally reliable and valid. The more appropriate conclusion is that the extent of participation is low in a study (B) based on data which were relatively reliable and valid, but it was high in another study (A) which was based on data of questionable reliability and validity. In essence, more weight is given to study B than to study A.

ASSUMING THAT THE SAME VARIABLE IS DEFINED IDENTICALLY IN DIFFERENT STUDIES

A receiver of research communications about different studies which include the same variable should not automatically assume that the variable is defined identically in all of the studies. Such an assumption is potentially abusive. Suppose two studies are conducted to describe correlates of juvenile delinquency. One study, C, operationally defines juvenile delinquency as the number of juveniles between the ages of 8 and 18 who appear in court because of offenses punishable in accordance with the law. Another study, D, may operationally define juvenile delinquency as the number of persons attending junior and senior high schools who indicate, when responding to a questionnaire, that they have engaged in offenses punishable by law. The two definitions are clearly different, yet they are intended to represent the variable of juvenile delinquency.

An abuse could occur if one regards the results of study C as comparable to those of study D. For example, study C may indicate that low socioeconomic status is a correlate of juvenile delinquency, while a low self concept is a correlate of juvenile delinquency in study D. An erroneous conclusion derived from those two studies would be that *both* low economic status and a low self concept are correlates of juvenile delinquency. Further analysis might reveal that in study C there is no association between a low self concept and juvenile delinquency, and in study D there is no association between low economic status and juvenile delinquency.

EMPLOYING FALSE CRITERIA OF CAUSALITY

Receivers of research communications often make inappropriate inferences about causal relationships between variables. There are two types of errors made by invoking false criteria of causality: 1) assuming that a relationship is causal when there is insufficient evidence; 2) assuming that a relationship is not causal, also on the basis of incomplete evidence.

The first type of error occurs when *all* of the criteria for causality (the causal variable preceding the effect variable in time, a correlation between the causal [independent] variable and the effect [dependent] variable, other variables that could affect the relationship being ruled out as contributing factors, and the relationship being empirically generalizable) are not invoked. Thus, an abuse is the equation of any *one* of the criteria for causality with causality (having all of the criteria). Perhaps, the most common error is that of equating correlation with causation.[25] For example, suppose there is a high correlation between clients' liking of caseworkers and their continuance in casework treatment. One would erroneously infer from that correlation that if caseworkers get clients to like them more, the clients will continue for longer periods of time in casework treatment. This is because there is incomplete information about the other criteria necessary for inferring causality. Other variables may also be highly correlated with continuance—the nature of the clients' problems, the amount of fees that they may have to pay for services, the perceived competence of the caseworkers, and client and caseworker characteristics such as age, sex, etc.

The second type of error is the converse of the first type. That is, one could not infer that a relationship is *not* causal on the basis of incomplete evidence. Thus, there may be (or may not be) a causal relationship between clients' liking of caseworkers and continuance in treatment; and it is erroneous to assume there is not a causal relationship until one has the necessary information regarding all of the criteria for causality.

Related to that error is the false criterion of noncausality enunciated by Hirschi and Selvin: "Insofar as a relation between two variables is not perfect, the relation is not causal." [26] A nonperfect correlation is, in general, a correlation that is less than 1, but greater than 0. Suppose the relationship between two variables, x and y, is .80. It would be erroneous to infer that the relationship is not causal. This is because there may be multiple causation, that is, both x and w, for example, may interact to cause variable y. The error in inference is to assume that causation is necessarily restricted to the relationship between two variables. Hence, continuance may be a result of the combined influence of clients' liking of caseworkers, the nature of the clients' problems, etc.

Another false criterion of noncausality is that the independent variable is not causal if its relation to the dependent variable is contingent upon other variables.[27] This criterion is inaccurate because it also implies that multiple causation is not possible. Suppose that there is a high correlation between clients' liking of caseworkers and continuance in treatment; and in further analysis it is shown that the correlation only holds for clients of agencies which do not require clients to continue unless they choose to do so. The correlation between the independent variable of "liking" and the dependent variable, "continuance," is contingent upon the type of social agency. It would be erroneous to infer that the relationship is not causal; it may be causal, but only for specific types of agencies.[28]

Abuses in the Implementation of Research Knowledge

There are social research abuses that take place after social work practitioners have accurately received research communications relevant for social work practice. Obviously, it is inappropriate to use social research results which either are not pertinent to social work tasks and functions, or are of questionable accuracy. Therefore, abuses in the implementation of research knowledge refer to intentional distortions of usable knowledge from social research, rather than to errors in the understanding of research communications. These abuses are blinding, inertia, eye-wash, white-wash, and hog-wash.

BLINDING

Blinding is the act of filing away communications of research findings for posterity. The purpose of blinding by an administrator is to keep potentially relevant information away from the staff in a social agency so that it will not have to be considered for possible implementation. Suppose research is conducted on a social agency, and it indicates the following: administrators have not deployed their staff and resources efficiently; the agency has not achieved its objectives regarding the alleviation of clients' problems; and staff turnover is high, and staff morale is low. If an administrator keeps such results away from the staff, it is abusive because it is not in accordance with the social workers' stance of accountability to continually improve services for their clientele. Of course, some research reports might be filed away because it is believed that they are worthless. Nevertheless, the results of research should be made public. Whereas an administrator might regard the research as useless, a staff person(s) might regard it as useful—at least in the sense of specifying problems with which the agency must deal.

Blinding can also occur when an individual keeps information away from himself. For example, a social caseworker who employs a particular mode of treatment may have received the following types of knowledge: his treatment modality appears to be ineffective for achieving client goals; other types of intervention appear to be more effective and efficient. That caseworker may file away such knowledge so that he does not have to consider the possibility of changing his techniques. If he can keep the knowledge "out of sight," he hopes that it will also be kept "out of mind."

INERTIA

Inertia is the failure to implement relevant research findings regarding social work practice. It may occur when the social worker has not succeeded in suppressing pertinent knowledge through the process of blinding. Thus, the social worker would acknowledge the importance of the research results, but he (or his agency, or a larger organization) does not attempt to implement them. Suppose, for example, that a number of research studies have consistently demonstrated that matching characteristics of adoptive children with those of prospective, adoptive parents is time-consuming, and is not related to the extent to which adoptive children will function adequately with their adoptive parents, i.e., criteria employed in selecting adoptive parents are unrelated to the social adjustment of adoptive children. An administrator and his staff may believe that the knowledge is accurate and relevant, yet they may continue to employ the same criteria for selecting adoptive parents. If no attempts are made to change those procedures—given that they have confidence in the research knowledge and they are accountable to their clientele—then those social workers would be abusing research knowledge.

EYE-WASH

Eye-wash is the attempt to select only those positive or negative aspects of research findings that relate to the work of an individual, group, program, or organization.[29] The person who wishes to make a program "look good" selects positive features of the research, while one who wishes to undermine a program would select only negative aspects of the research findings. For example, a study of community organization may indicate that a large number of people participated in meetings which were held to discuss issues in local government. That might be interpreted as "positive" in that it is in favor of the community organizers. Further information from the research study may show that the attendance at meetings declined rapidly; such information could be construed as "negative." Thus, a more positive picture of the effectiveness of community organization efforts emerges if one omits or ignores the information about a decline in attendance.

A different example pertains to a program which essentially has produced positive results. For instance, a drug abuse program may have been successful in contacting a large number of drug addicts and in engaging them with the program workers. The drug addicts may have reduced their intake of drugs, and they may have secured jobs and education that they did not have prior to their involvement in the program. Staff morale may be high, but the use of staff persons may be somewhat inefficient in that too much time is spent in clerical rather than in direct service activities. Surely, if one highlights information about inefficiency and ignores knowledge of program effectiveness, the program would "look worse" than it actually is.

WHITE-WASH

An abuse which is closely related to eye-wash is that of white-wash. This abuse occurs often in evaluations of social programs and, according to Suchman, white-wash is "an attempt to cover up program failure or errors by avoiding any objective appraisal." [30] In this type of abuse, an administrator employs testimonials from selected persons who are in favor of his program. One uses the process of blinding to discard or ignore results from research studies based on relatively reliable and objective data. Then, he seeks testimonials from program recipients who he knows are in favor of the program. For example, suppose that a group work program has an objective of developing "self concepts" in unwed, teenage mothers. Suppose further that the results of a research study indicate that two out of three "mothers" felt that the group sessions were meaningless; they led to endless talk, and the group workers appeared to be self-righteous and condescending. In addition, no changes in self concept were observed, and attendance among the group members dropped considerably after the first several sessions. The abuser employing the technique of white-wash would locate several clients who liked the group workers and the program; in fact, the clients may even be hired by the program as paraprofessional aides. Each of the respondents is asked to make statements pertaining to their satisfactions in the program. Favorable testimonials are then used to represent program progress, while the research results are discarded.

HOG-WASH

Hog-wash is similar to the abuse of posture that was discussed previously in the section on abuses in the initiation of social research.[31] It refers to a deliberate misleading of other social work practitioners by fostering an image of objectivity. For example, a program director may indicate that certain changes have been made in his program, and that research is a continuous activity in which all staff members are involved. The intent is to mislead others into believing that changes are made on the basis of research. Others are not informed about the real reasons for change (e.g., political pressures, changes in available funds and resources, or changes in values); and it is hoped that the image of an "objective, accountable program" is fostered.

Of course, hog-wash can also take place among individuals. For example, a group worker may indicate to a colleague that he tape records all of his sessions, and he systematically compiles information about his activities as a group worker. At the same time, he says that he is switching to a more "effective" procedure for structuring his groups. The "more effective" procedure may be based on the group worker's changing values or on an idea he has obtained in his reading. Moreover, the group worker may simply collect information, without attempting to analyze it in relation to his new procedures. The abuse again is one of fostering an image of change that is supposed to be based on research findings.

Chapter 6

Facilitating Research Utilization

We have emphasized that research utilization would be enhanced if the communication gaps between social researchers and social workers were minimized. Obviously, the simplest solution to the problem of research utilization is to insist that social work practitioners get extensive training in research methodology, and conduct their own research. Such a solution is analogous to that of the training that clinical psychologists receive in theory, practice, and research. This implies more education for social workers—a Ph.D. or DSW degree. Most social work practitioners and students, however, prefer to engage in direct service or policy and administrative activities, rather than in social research. In essence, although the idea of training all social workers to be researchers in their own practice is desirable, the prospects for the attainment of that particular goal are bleak. To be sure, there are social workers who are interested in both practice and research, but the realities are that most social work jobs leave little time for research, and support for research through social agencies and organizations is not extensive. Consequently, scholars in social work and social research have suggested that research utilization might best be facilitated through increased collaboration between researchers and practitioners.[1] Therefore, it is necessary to identify a number of possible ways in which research utilization might be enhanced through varying degrees of research-practitioner collaboration.

Two main areas could lead to an increased utilization of social research: the conduct of practice-related research, and the conduct of research utilization activities. The former is concerned with a specification of planned social research efforts that can result in knowledge directly applicable to social work practice; while the latter is devoted to mechanisms by which practitioners can create models for research utilization.

The Conduct of Practice-Related Research

Practice-related research is research planned to be relevant for practice. It involves administrators, policy makers, and / or direct service practitioners, in addition to researchers dealing with problems of social work practice. To suggest possible modes of practice-related research, five different but interrelated types are presented: experimental social innovation; planning and evaluation surveys; research, development, training, and evaluation; utilization, research, and development; and practice development and research. These practice-research modes were selected for two primary reasons: 1) they illustrate the potential for planning practice-related research; 2) these types are currently being employed in practice.

EXPERIMENTAL SOCIAL INNOVATION

Experimental social innovation is the use of experimental methods for testing policy or practice alternatives specified by policy developers and administrators.[2] Alternatives are delineated, plans are made for their operationalization, the various alternatives are experimentally manipulated and necessary administrative arrangements for researchers and practitioners are made, data pertaining to the relative effectiveness and efficiency of the alternatives are obtained, the results are processed and analyzed, the interpretations of results are discussed by policy developers and researchers, and, finally, the results are used as inputs for making decisions concerning the further implementation of those alternatives.

An alternative is simply a choice among one or more plans, strategies, or procedures. Policy makers in family casework agencies, for example, may specify several alternatives concerned with the optimal duration of social work intervention for couples with marital problems: one month, several months, one year, or unlimited time duration. Experimental social innovation might be employed to test the relative effectiveness and efficiency of those time-constrained alternatives. Examples of practice-research questions that lead to the testing of other alternatives are as follows: Which procedure is more effective: providing intervention for delinquents in closed settings (alternative A), or in open settings (alternative B)? Which form of supervision is most effective with nonprofessional workers: group supervision (alternative A), or individual supervision (alternative B)? To what extent would persons from a particular ethnic group utilize health and welfare services: if the professional practitioners are from the same ethnic group (alternative A), or from different ethnic groups (alternative B)?

When there are clear alternatives that can be specified in advance of the research, it is possible to test them by experimental procedures.[3] Moreover, experimental social innovations can provide inputs for decision-making—especially when they are devised to answer policy questions framed by persons who have the power and authority to make or to influence decisions.

There is currently much interest in various types of reform for systems of income maintenance. In this regard, the Office of the Secretary of Health, Education, and Welfare (HEW) has been undertaking a number of experiments in different communities to provide answers to questions such as: what are the effects of different work incentive plans with respect to the reduction of the number of welfare recipients?

One of these experiments is taking place in Gary, Indiana: 800 poor persons receive regular transfer payments semi-monthly from the Gary Income Maintenance Project, and a control group of 800 poor families do not (although they may receive assistance from other programs).[4] In addition, one experimental subgroup is provided day care services with no requirement to seek work, while the families in another subgroup must seek work in order to receive day care services. Hence, a number of alternatives are being manipulated to determine which ones are more likely to result in increased employment, reduction of persons on the welfare rolls, greater family stability, and better educational achievements for children from families who receive AFDC payments. It is assumed that such information would be used by HEW and Congress to make decisions regarding income maintenance plans.

The essence of experimental social innovation is that research is employed to test the relative efficacy of different alternatives specified by policy makers. The alternatives are manipulated in pilot experimental programs, prior to their possible implementation in large-scale programs. Thus, it is planned that the results of the research will be utilized as inputs for making choices among various policy and practice alternatives, and there is, ideally, collaboration between policy makers and researchers— from the initiation of research to the interpretation and potential utilization of research results. It should be noted, however, that policy and practice decisions are not necessarily based on information obtained through rational procedures such as experimental social innovation. Policy decisions may be influenced by politics, pressure groups, public sentiments, costs, etc.[5] Although experimental social innovation can aid in the decision-making process, it will not be of value unless policy makers and administrators believe in its potential and are willing to use the results of such research.

Planning and evaluation surveys involve the use of survey methods for gathering information directly related to the establishment of new social programs or practice approaches or to the modification of existing programs. These surveys are conducted by administrators, social planners, and their staffs; by researchers located within or outside the organizations interested in survey information; or by survey centers or private research organizations commissioned to conduct surveys for administrators and social planners. There are five interrelated uses of survey methods that bear directly on social planning for social agencies and organizations: need surveys, eligibility surveys, resource surveys, service utilization surveys, and evaluation surveys.[6]

Need surveys are surveys conducted to identify the health, educational, and social needs of client and potential client populations.[7] "Needs" may pertain to economic assistance, adequate housing, medical assistance, family counseling, budget planning, legal aid, psychological problems, recreation, and so forth. A need survey is often conducted prior to the establishment of new programs to determine the kind and extent of services that might be most suitable for a specific population. Thus, an agency that attempts to gear its services to the poor (or to the "elderly," or to potential delinquents, etc.) may plan for a survey which has the purpose of obtaining information about the expressed wishes, desires, and problems of economically deprived families. Low-income families included in the survey population may be most interested, for example, in obtaining sufficient income to increase their standards of living, adequate medical and dental care, and low-cost, legal assistance. Based on that information, a social agency may decide to increase its efforts in establishing information and referral services to employment, medical, and legal aid programs, and to provide mechanisms for helping clients to receive the necessary assistance from those programs.

Eligibility surveys are conducted to determine the extent to which persons are eligible for a program, or the amount of funds that should be allocated to a program on the basis of those persons who are potentially eligible for it. Typically, programs are already available, and eligibility surveys are conducted to identify potential program beneficiaries. Censuses of local areas are important for social planners because monies allocated for social programs often depend on the number of persons living in those areas and, in particular, on the number of persons who have identifiable characteristics necessary for the receipt of program funds. For example, funds for Office of Economic Opportunity (OEO) programs have been allocated to different areas proportionate to the number of low-income families residing in those areas. Funds for literacy programs depend on populations (or subpopulations) of illiterate persons, as determined by criteria established by the policy makers of those programs. A program providing recreational facilities for a population of "senior citizens" needs to identify those elderly persons who require the services of the program.

Resource surveys are conducted for the purpose of determining whether there are available services congruent with the needs of a client population. Such surveys are carried out by administrators, social planners, and/or social researchers to locate and develop rosters of resources (public and private agencies, foundations, organizations, lists of volunteers, etc.), and to obtain information about the extent to which those resources could be employed for meeting the needs of client populations.

"Needs" represent the "demand" for services, while "resources" indicate the "supply" available for meeting those demands. If the resources are fewer than the needs, additional services are necessary, whereas an overabundance of resources in relation to needs may indicate that programs should be modified (to meet other "needs") or abolished. Hence, resource surveys are complementary to need surveys, and provide important information necessary for making decisions about social programs.

Service utilization surveys are conducted to determine the extent to which those "in need" are cognizant of and actually use (or would use) resources available to them.[8] These surveys overlap with need, eligibility, and resource surveys; in fact, all four types of surveys may be conducted simultaneously to provide a picture of the extent of need, the resources available to meet those needs, the persons eligible for existing services, the extent to which eligible persons know about available services, and the conditions under which those persons would actually utilize existing services or new programs. Such information is vital for administrators, program directors, and social planners.

For example, a low-income, Spanish-speaking population might be eligible for an Operation Headstart program aimed at increasing the readiness of pre-school children for school. The families may know that their children are eligible for Operation Headstart, but they do not enroll their children in the program. A service utilization survey may reveal that those families do not utilize the program because none of the teachers are able to speak Spanish and communicate adequately with the children and their parents. That information may lead to the hiring of bilingual teachers who may be able to communicate with the parents, and who might be more capable of preparing the Spanish-speaking children for schools in which English is spoken. Moreover, that information may stimulate social workers to advocate classes in the schools which are specifically devoted to Spanish-speaking children.

Evaluation surveys utilize survey methods for providing information about the relative successes and failures of social programs, practices, and policies.[9] Such information is ideally employed as inputs for decisions about the expansion, modification, or contraction of social programs. An evaluation survey has the same purpose as experimental social innovation, but it is different in that the researcher does not manipulate and have control over program interventions, and the survey is conducted after a program is in operation. Thus, evaluation surveys may be conducted to serve as quasi-experiments with comparative, correlational, and *ex post facto* research designs.[10]

An example of this kind of survey is an evaluation of the social security disability program. The survey was initiated by HEW and contracted out to researchers at Johns Hopkins University. The purpose of the study was to

> . . . examine the post-evaluation experience of a group of applicants denied disability benefits (cases) and to contrast their experiences with a group of applicants allowed benefits (controls). It includes an analysis of the current medical, vocational, and socioeconomic status of the two groups of disability applicants. The findings will provide some objective measure of the efficacy and accuracy of the guides used in benefit determinations.[11]

The study was conducted with a sample of 1,564 persons from 1964 to 1966. Two types of information were sought: a physical examination in hospital clinics, and interviews inquiring about disabilities and illnesses, employment, utilization of medical and rehabilitative services, and so forth. The researchers produced data indicating that the program process for evaluating persons (as eligible for disability benefits) was effective in that it screened out persons who were severely disabled from those who were less disabled. They pointed out, however, that there was turnover in those who were in the study group, and that the program needed some sort of "systematic recall and reassessment procedure" to evaluate adequately changes in the status of applicants from time to time. The researchers also indicated that there was a lack of continuity between the evaluative process and the utilization of physical and rehabilitative services. The research report was distributed to administrators and policy makers within HEW, and it was also made available to others interested in the social security disability program. Thus, an evaluation study of the social security disability program was commissioned by HEW, and the results of the research were disseminated to persons who develop policy and implement the program.

RESEARCH, DEVELOPMENT, TRAINING, AND EVALUATION

This mode of practice-related research is comprised of four interrelated features. First, research is focused on several aspects of social work practice. The research is conceived and executed by a team of researchers and practitioners. Second, those aspects of practice which have empirical support (from the research) are described so that they can be used for training purposes, Third, the research-practice staff develops a training program, and trains other practitioners. Fourth, the training is evaluated.

An example of this approach is the Family and School Consultation Project, directed by Dr. Richard B. Stuart and funded by the National Institutes of Health.[12] Based on previous uses of principles of behavior modification in practice and research with delinquent adolescents, a set of procedures was developed by the project staff for intervention with predelinquent youth in junior high schools. The staff, comprised of social work practitioners and researchers trained in the use of behavior modification, developed a variety of procedures for modifying behaviors through interventions with adolescents, their families, and school personnel. Their procedures include the formation of contracts with privileges, sanctions, bonuses, and responsibilities; applications of principles of positive reinforcement for increasing positive family interactions; the use of tokens, monitoring, feedback mechanisms, etc. The project is concerned with a variety of practice-research questions such as the following: What is the optimal length of time for rendering treatment based on positive reinforcement and on an interpersonal interactional perspective of behavior? At what points in the treatment should such techniques as the use of tokens for the reinforcement of positive family interaction be employed? What is the relative effectiveness and efficiency of different types of contracts between predelinquent youth and their families, e.g., contracts negotiated between the family members as compared with contracts negotiated by therapists (social work practitioners) and the family?

The project staff devised several research designs to test the efficacy of different intervention procedures. One design, for example, was focused on an "Experimental Evaluation of Three Time-Constrained Behavioral Treatments for Predelinquents and Delinquents." [13] The results of treatment, prescribed to terminate in 15, 45, or 90 days, were studied in a pre-test/post-test comparison group design. Treatment was provided for those junior high-school students who had behavioral problems in school, and whose families were willing to participate in the project. Data were collected on school performance, social behavior at home, community adjustment in terms of juvenile court contacts, and attitude changes in relation to delinquency. The experiment was conducted for one year, 1970–1971, with 80 junior high-school students, and follow-up data are still being collected. Preliminary analyses indicated that the 15-day treatment was the most efficient in terms of cost, and was as effective as either the 45- or 90-day treatment conditions.

A second experiment devised by the Family and School Consultation Project is a factorial design involving the comparison of two different lengths of treatment time, family negotiated contracts vs. fixed contracts, and fading (planned reduction of therapist-client contacts—from interviews to phone calls to termination) vs. non-fading procedures. The purpose of such comparisons is to locate the most effective alternatives in relation to a variety of behavioral and attitudinal measures. The experiment was also carried out for one year, 1971–1972, and it was planned that follow-up data would be collected for a period of two years. Other research efforts in the project involve the comparison of behavior modification with activity-group discussions, and studies of the relationship of measures of therapist-client interactions to client outcomes.

The Family and School Consultation Project is currently in the research phase of its operations. Its overall plan is to follow the model of research, development, training, and evaluation. In the research phase a series of interrelated research-practice efforts are formulated and tested by the project staff. The purpose of the research is to enable the project staff to make informed judgments about the relative efficacy and efficiency of their procedures. Those procedures that appear to be most effective will then be specified as precisely as possible. This is facilitated by video-taping of interviews, monitoring forms, records of therapists' instigatory activities in interviews, records of treatment contracts, and staff discussions. Subsequently, it is planned to develop films, pamphlets, and manuals to be used for training other professionals. The staff would develop a series of training sessions in order to communicate that technology which is most effective. Finally, the effectiveness of training would be evaluated for the purpose of devising those methods most suitable for disseminating the knowledge derived from the project.

This model of practice-related research is analogous to the research and development models used in engineering, business, and industry, and to Havelock's research, development, and diffusion perspective for disseminating knowledge about innovations in practice.[14] Of course, positive results may not always be forthcoming from such research, for the researchers may find that the practice procedures are not effective. If so, a training program based on effective intervention strategies could not be developed. Nevertheless, the approach is promising because it could lead to the development of a technology based on empirical evidence obtained through social research.

UTILIZATION, RESEARCH, AND DEVELOPMENT

Utilization, research, and development (URD) is an approach that is closely related to that of research, development, training, and evaluation (RDTE). The primary difference is in the formulation of hypotheses for research. While RDTE formulates hypotheses which may be based on knowledge from previous research studies, it is not dependent on a systematic review of the research literature for the articulation of those hypotheses. In contrast, URD is predicated on a relatively thorough analysis of the available research literature. First, the researchers attempt to utilize literature which bears on social work. This is done, for example, by reviewing a variety of journals and books with respect to the validity of previous research knowledge and the articulation of principles for social work practice. Research is then devised to assess how far those hypotheses ("practice principles") are useful for social work practitioners. Finally, those principles that can be used successfully by social work practitioners are codified and summarized, e.g., in a training manual.

This approach is exemplified by the research efforts of Jack Rothman and his staff at the Social Work Center of the University of Michigan School of Social Work. Rothman's research is devoted to utilizing social science research for the purpose of developing guidelines for community practice and social planning.[15] The first phase of the research involved a systematic study of social science research reports that were related to social change. In that study, Rothman and his associates employed the following procedures for locating relevant literature:

> The major retrieval approach entailed a thorough detailed search of a selected group of thirty journals which had been found to contain, in relatively large proportions, the kinds of data being sought. These journals were examined rigorously over the six-year period, 1964–70. Sociological journals received emphasis in coverage, although other fields were also included—political science, applied anthropology, psychology, social psychology, and the journals of several professional practice fields.
>
> The journals selected for study were those which contained proportionately larger numbers of articles that have the following characteristics:
>   a. empirical research findings.
>   b. community context or community change variables.
>   c. an applied emphasis or potential action derivatives—either directly or indirectly.
>
> The general rule was to seek out articles that were fairly close to the "stuff" of community practice or whose findings could be applied fairly readily and obviously to community practice. Preference was given to evaluative studies of change projects, studies of community planning, committee processes, *investigation of participation* in civic action and voluntary associations, etc.[16]

In addition, the research staff reviewed doctoral dissertations, professional papers, books, and reports. Over 900 research studies were reviewed, and a large number of propositions (generalizations of research knowledge) and action guidelines were formulated in relation to selected areas such as the "organizational setting for intervention" and "citizen participation." [17] The following format was employed for presenting each proposition: the proposition is articulated; research studies compatible with the proposition are listed; the research staff's confidence (ranging from low confidence to high confidence, and based on empirical support for the proposition) in the proposition is indicated; and action guidelines are delineated for subsequent research.

The Rothman project is currently in the second phase, which involves a testing of the action guidelines in social work practice settings.[18] Community practitioners are hired to work with the researchers to select guidelines that can be tried out, and research is designed for gathering data related to the practitioner's experiences in employing the guidelines. By using community practitioners in a variety of social work settings, it is hoped to obtain generalizable results about the use of action guidelines. Finally, it is planned to spell out the various conditions in which guidelines can (or cannot) be applied in practice.

PRACTICE DEVELOPMENT AND RESEARCH

Practice development and research involves both practitioners and researchers in case studies of new practice modalities. The primary objectives of the research are to systematize experiences in developing practice interventions, and to formulate hypotheses for research. This mode of practice-related research is especially useful when practitioners do not have well-developed theories or practical guidelines for conducting their work.

An example of a practice development and research project is that of the Riverdale Community Organization, which is located in a metropolitan community.[19] There, the community organizers are particularly interested in devising strategies and procedures for getting community residents involved in identifying and dealing with relevant issues, such as the availability of parking space, housing, etc. More limited goals of the community organization efforts are to develop and maintain active participation among the residents, and to assist them in formulating plans for community action.

The practice development and research approach planned by that project includes the following features:

1. Every community organizer records his daily activities with respect to his organizing plans, expectations, attempts, and outcomes. These chronological logs are reviewed weekly by the organizers and by the people being organized (organizees).
2. An evaluation panel made up of researchers, community

organizers, and organizees, develops a system for recording only those data that appear to be related to the tasks and functions of the organization, such as committee meetings, organization meetings, and publicity campaigns.

3. Selected group meetings are video-taped so that interaction processes of leaders, potential leaders, and followers can be studied through content analyses.

4. As the project unfolds, data regarding attendance, participation, attitudes, and outcomes of group meetings are discussed by the evaluation panel. Hypotheses are then developed for application in subsequent group meetings.

The purpose of these procedures is to help both the organizers and the organizees to generate potentially useful strategies. As the project gains experience as to what strategies appear to be effective (or ineffective) for specific situations, the evaluation panel suggests modifications for practice and new modes for gathering data related to those modifications. The net result is a documentation of the trial-and-error process that may be involved in that particular kind of community organization. Some procedures for eliciting participation may rarely work, while others may be repeatedly effective—irrespective of the community issue, or of the characteristics of the organizers and the organizees. Such systematic documentation provides an overview of the community organization's experiences, and it also enables the organizers to be accountable to each other for their perceived successes and failures. As the intervention efforts become more standardized, in that the activities of the organizers become more amenable to specification, research can be devised for testing hypotheses about the impact of community organization practice.

The Conduct of Research Utilization

In the final analysis, social work practitioners (administrators, social planners, community organizers, social caseworkers, and social group workers) are instrumental in determining whether or not research knowledge will be used in social work. Hence, it is assumed in this concluding section that the use of social research will be enhanced if practitioners take an active role in developing research utilization schemes. Five interrelated modalities for increasing research utilization efforts are identified: organizational facilitation, research utilization workshops, reviews of research, consultants in utilization development roles, and research utilization skills through education.

ORGANIZATIONAL FACILITATION

Organizational facilitation is the extent to which social agencies, organizations, schools, and professional associations provide the means by which the process of utilization can occur. Within and among social agencies and organizations, utilization can be facilitated by activities such as the following: encouragement of utilization efforts, development of working committees to review research knowledge relating to the needs of clients, workers, and social agencies, provision of staff time for working on utilization, and provision of resources for the staff and for consultants who might help social workers in their utilization endeavors.[20]

Schools of social work can promote utilization in at least three ways. First, faculty members and students can devote some of their efforts to generating knowledge about effective modalities for increasing research utilization skills. Second, courses on using research knowledge in particular substantive areas can be developed and taught. Third, conferences and workshops pertaining to the use of research knowledge can be sponsored for social work practitioners.*

Professional associations, such as the National Association of Social Workers, may encourage research utilization by the following means:

1. The development of sections of national conferences which deal with the utilization of social research knowledge that bears on particular areas of social work practice.[21]

2. The formation of national committees devoted to generat-

* Such activities have taken place at the University of Michigan School of Social Work.

ing models for using research knowledge. The committees would be comprised of practitioners, researchers, and educators, and provisions would be made so that their findings would be communicated to the national membership.

3. The stimulation and coordination of utilization efforts that can be carried out by local chapters of the professional association.

4. The solicitation of financial resources for encouraging practitioners and researchers to collaborate in devising utilization strategies.

5. The simultaneous publication of research and utilization articles in professional journals. For example, a research report would be followed by one or more articles by practitioners with respect to their potential uses of the research findings. Moreover, the views of the readers regarding the potential or actual uses of the research knowledge could be solicited and published. This might increase the involvement of those practitioners who read most of the articles in professional journals, but often skip research reports.

The preceding suggestions are based on the basic assumption that social workers are interested in research utilization, and recognize it as an important professional activity.[22] Although many of these suggestions have been employed on a small scale, it is the view of the author that utilization efforts have not been sufficiently encouraged and promoted by the profession of social work. If utilization of research has a low priority in social agencies and organizations, then it is unlikely that available research knowledge will be effectively used. In this respect, the reader should refer to chapter 3 for an analysis of dimensions pertinent to using social research knowledge.

RESEARCH UTILIZATION WORKSHOPS

Research utilization workshops are conducted for the purposes of understanding research knowledge and disseminating it to practitioners, researchers, and educators, and for developing methods for its application. Workshops are comprised of small groups of social workers who meet for short periods of time—ranging from a couple of hours in one session to several sessions over a one- or two-week period. They may be held in postgraduate institutes, conferences, universities, social agencies, and other organizations.

Although little attention has been devoted by the social work profession to conducting workshops exclusively geared to research utilization for practitioners, two types of workshop are discernible: those concerned with the process of utilization, and those dealing with the utilization of specific forms of research knowledge for particular practice areas.

Workshops focused on the process of utilization may be devoted to such issues as the following: 1) What are the most effective ways to enhance communications between researchers and practitioners? 2) How can practice needs be identified, and how can the results of available research be used to help meet those practice needs? 3) What kinds of research would be most directly related to the needs of practitioners and their clients and how can such research be facilitated? 4) How necessary is it for practitioners to use verified knowledge? To what extent are social workers accountable to their clientele regarding knowledge about social work interventions?

These issues can be discussed in workshops comprised of researchers, practitioners, and clients. The presence of clients (or ex-clients) in those discussions may help social work practitioners and social researchers to develop more realistic plans for employing research results in practice. Moreover, practitioners can learn more about research through interactions with researchers, and researchers can become more sensitized to the problems of practitioners.

Research utilization workshops that deal with the application of specific forms of research knowledge may be focused on such topics as: 1) What research results are available regarding the substantive area of the workshop? 2) What practice principles and techniques can be derived from the research findings? 3) How could those practice techniques be implemented? 4) How could the effectiveness of those procedures be evaluated in specific intervention situations?

An example of that type of utilization workshop is apparent in the work of Frank Maple of the University of Michigan School of Social Work, who has conducted a number of workshops to train school social workers. In one workshop held at a high school, the participants were the administrative staff, teachers, social workers, and pupils.[23] The topic was the use of data obtained from students in a classroom for developing strategies to increase student participation. First, research bearing on student participation and classroom management was reviewed by Maple and discussed by the participants. Second, practice principles derived from the research were articulated and discussed. Third, a demonstration of the use of those principles was conducted within a classroom of the school regarded by the teacher as one with low student participation. Students were asked to indicate their extent of participation in class, i.e., whether it was low or high. In that particular class, the students indicated that their participation was low, verifying the teacher's observations. The students and the teacher were then asked to indicate what the students most desired, and it was revealed that students wanted more free time in the classroom. A contract was subsequently negotiated between the students and the teacher. It specified that the students could earn approximately 20 minutes of free time during the day if they increased their classroom participation. This notion was based on principles derived from research on learning and classroom management. It was tried out, and evaluated with respect to the students' classroom participation and academic performance.

Maple showed how the techniques derived from research could be used in practice by *demonstrating* their use in a practical situation. The involvement of school personnel led to discussions which increased the likelihood of success for those intervention strategies. Thus, research utilization workshops can be devoted to training or staff development, and an effective mode of communication appears to be an actual demonstration of how to use the knowledge derived from the research.

Research reviews are carried out by social work scholars for the following purposes: to summarize consistent research findings within substantive knowledge areas; to indicate gaps in knowledge and to identify areas for further research; to specify problems in research methodology and to point to the need for new research methods; and to delineate social research knowledge that could be employed by practitioners.[24]

Typically, the reviews are written by scholars and read by other scholars. Although the extent to which social work practitioners read research reviews is unknown, it is probable that the bulk of social workers do not read research reviews. This may be because of two primary reasons: 1) The reviews may not be addressed systematically to the problems and needs of social work practitioners, but may rather be written for educators, theoreticians, and social researchers for the purpose of highlighting research rather than practice issues; 2) The information contained within the reviews may not be sufficiently disseminated—review articles are usually found in books and professional journals, and other communication channels such as workshops, conferences, and the use of consultants may not be effectively utilized.

Research reviews in conjunction with other modalities for disseminating and utilizing research knowledge can be useful for social work practitioners, especially if the research reviews are devoted to the articulation of actual and potential uses of the research knowledge in social work settings. This can be facilitated by the participation of practitioners in the review process and by the conscious efforts of reviewers to present their findings to the large audience of practicing social workers. Moreover, effective models for presenting research findings within research reviews might be developed.

Kadushin's review of research in child welfare is an example of a model for presenting substantive knowledge to social workers. He indicated what areas of child welfare he focused on and the sources for his review: empirical research reports in the areas of adoption, foster family care, and institutional child care in the United States and England from 1964 to 1969. In particular, he focused his review on "the child in interaction with a social situation that necessitates his being cared for and protected by persons other than his natural parents." [25] For each of the areas that he reviewed (such as adoption), he systematically followed this format. First, policy problems and issues were articulated. Second, a number of research studies which bear on those issues were evaluated. Third, consistent findings (and inconsistent results) were summarized. Fourth, practice implications were derived from those research results.

Other models for presenting research reviews could be formulated, and more attention could be focused on the process of communicating such knowledge to social workers. A step in this direction is the publication of research reviews in selected areas of social work by the National Association of Social Workers.[26] Future efforts might be devoted to determining the extent to which those reviews are actually read, and to consider how they could be more related to direct practice activities.

CONSULTANTS IN UTILIZATION DEVELOPMENT ROLES

Consultants can help social agencies and organizations to effectively use social research by serving in one or more of several interrelated capacities, e.g., as researcher, trainer, interpreter, and/or utilization facilitator. In the role of researcher, the consultant helps the organization develop research that bears on agency problems. Included in the researcher's function is the planning of mechanisms to provide feedback to the organization with respect to the results of the research. Such mechanisms might consist of group meetings with administrators and practitioners for planning, conducting, analyzing, and interpreting the research; lectures and discussions on selected aspects of research methodology; considerations of data-processing procedures for disseminating tabulations of data; and the planning, production, and distribution of research reports that can be understood by the staff of the organization. In essence, this is the role of the applied researcher in social settings, with emphasis being placed on collaboration between researchers and practitioners for the primary objective of producing knowledge that can be used by practitioners.[27]

Consultants can also function as trainers. A trainer is an expert in an area of knowledge who is able to disseminate that knowledge by means of lectures, seminars, demonstrations, training institutes, workshops, and so forth. The trainer reviews and digests research results that are pertinent to his area of expertise and trains others to understand and to use such knowledge. Referring to the previous discussion of research utilization workshops, it is noted that Maple functioned as a trainer in conducting a workshop on classroom management. Thus, trainers can facilitate research utilization by employing their skills in involving groups of practitioners in the process of utilizing research.

Another consultant role is that of interpreter. An interpreter is skilled in translating the language of research into language that is more compatible with social work practice.[28] This requires that the consultant understand the methodologies and problems of social work practice and social research. Such roles may be developed by schools of social work, and by the creation of jobs in social work which utilize those skills. Interpreters could assist in the production of periodicals, pamphlets, etc., geared to producing information that is communicable to practitioners, and they could also serve in training and research development capacities. In addition to disseminating research knowledge to practitioners, interpreters could also promulgate knowledge about social work practice to social researchers. Hence, the role of interpreter could be viewed as a facilitator of communication between practitioners and researchers.

Finally, consultants who are skilled in developing utilization strategies in specific practice settings could serve as utilization facilitators. They would help agencies and organizations develop their own mechanisms for utilizing research knowledge. Such consultants could instruct organizations in how to locate and evaluate available research knowledge. They could identify and present mechanisms for research utilization, and they could lead group discussions pertaining to the implementation of those mechanisms that might be appropriate for the organizations. Furthermore, strategies for developing practice-related hypotheses and for planning program evaluations could be generated.

In summary, research utilization consultants could be used for purposes of staff development, training, and research development. These consultants might be especially useful if social agencies are serious about generating and using new knowledge pertinent to social work. Of course, there are important practical considerations that are involved in an agency's use of consultants. For example, the use of consultants for the purpose of evaluating a social program involves a consideration of evaluation objectives, agency costs, the biases of the evaluation consultant, the commitment of the agency to change, etc.[29] Therefore, an effective use of research utilization consultants is more likely when social work practitioners are involved in selecting them and in determining what their contribution regarding the needs and priorities of social agencies should be.

RESEARCH UTILIZATION SKILLS THROUGH EDUCATION

The research utilization skills of social work students can be developed by means of formal education in schools of social work, e.g., in seminars, classes, and research utilization experiences related to field placements in social work practice. That research utilization is a topic of high priority in the teaching of social research to social work students is evident in a recent survey by Zimbalist and his associates.[30] It was found that an "understanding of basic research principles and procedures" and "the utilization of research by others" were almost unanimously regarded as highly important by the sixty-seven schools of social work that participated in the survey.

According to the perspective adopted in this book, research utilization skills include the following: developing channels for increasing researcher-practitioner communications, evaluating and reviewing research studies, determining whether research results and research methods can be employed in practice settings, implementing research knowledge in social work practice, and collaborating with researchers in formulating practice-related research studies. In addition to formal education through schools of social work, utilization skills could also be communicated to social workers by trainers in workshops and in inservice training institutes.

In conclusion, this book can be thought of as a modest attempt to present a point of view for developing the research utilization skills of social workers. I believe that knowledge from social research can be effectively used by facilitating communications between social researchers and social work practitioners, and by sensitizing social workers to the potential uses and abuses of social research knowledge.

Notes

~·~

Chapter 1. Social Research and Social Work

1. Tony Tripodi, Phillip Fellin, Irwin Epstein, and Roger Lind, eds., *Social Workers at Work: An Introduction to Social Work Practice* (Itasca, Ill., F. E. Peacock, 1972), Preface, pp. v–ix.

2. Some examples of major textbooks which use traditional designations of social work methods are as follows: Scott Briar and Henry Miller, *Problems and Issues in Social Casework* (New York, Columbia University Press, 1971); William Schwartz and Serapio R. Zalba, eds., *The Practice of Group Work* (New York, Columbia University Press, 1971); Fred M. Cox, John L. Erlich, Jack Rothman, and John E. Tropman, eds., *Strategies of Community Organization* (Itasca, Ill., F. E. Peacock, 1970); and Harry A. Schatz, ed., *Social Work Administration: A Resource Book* (New York, Council on Social Work Education, 1970).

3. For an exposition of different therapeutic techniques employed by social caseworkers, see Scott Briar and Henry Miller, and Robert W. Roberts and Robert H. Nee, eds., *Theories of Social Casework* (Chicago, University of Chicago Press, 1971).

4. A delineation of the tasks of social caseworkers is provided in Tony Tripodi et al., *Social Workers at Work*. Detailed descriptions of the functions and activities of social group workers, community organizers, administrators, and policy developers are also included.

5. See *ibid.*, pp. 2–10 and 56–107 for a variety of techniques employed by social group workers.

6. The ideas presented about the three modes of community practice are taken directly from this reference: Jack Rothman, "Three Models of Community Organization Practice," in Fred M. Cox et al., pp. 20–36.

7. Scott Briar and Henry Miller, p. 82.

8. Martin B. Loeb, "Evaluation as Accountability," in Leigh M. Roberts, Norman S. Greenfield, and Milton H. Miller, eds., *Comprehensive Mental Health: The Challenge of Evaluation* (Madison, University of Wisconsin Press, 1968), pp. 249–58.

9. Tony Tripodi, Phillip Fellin, and Irwin Epstein, *Social Program Evaluation* (Itasca, Ill.: F. E. Peacock, 1971), pp. 79–95.

10. Robert Morris, "Social Planning," in Henry S. Maas, ed., *Five Fields of Social Service: Reviews of Research* (New York, National Association of Social Workers, 1966), p. 186.

11. Roslyn Weinberger and Tony Tripodi, "Trends in Types of Research Reported in Selected Social Work Journals, 1956–65," *Social Service Review*, 43 (December 1969), 439–47; and Tony Tripodi, Fran Kaplan, and Phillip Fellin, "Evaluative Research in Social Work, 1960–1969," *Applied Social Studies* (in press).

12. For a review of literature related to the relationship of social researchers to social work practitioners, see Hyman Rodman and Ralph L. Kolodny, "Organizational Strains in the Researcher-Practitioner Relationship," in Alvin W. Gouldner and S. M. Miller, eds., *Applied Sociology: Opportunities and Problems* (New York, Free Press, 1965), pp. 93–114.

13. Scott Briar and Henry Miller, pp. 79–88.

14. Sidney Zimbalist, "Welfare Planning Research: Master or Servant" *Social Work*, 2 (July 1957), 40–44.

15. David Fanshel, ed., *Research in Social Welfare Administration: Its Contributions and Problems* (New York, National Association of Social Workers, 1962), pp. 84–120.

16. William Schwartz, "Neighborhood Centers and Group Work," in Henry S. Maas, ed., *Research in the Social Services: A Five-Year-Review* (New York, National Association of Social Workers, 1971), pp. 130–91; Sheldon D. Rose, "A Behavioral Approach to the Group Treatment of Parents," in Tony Tripodi et al., *Social Workers at Work* pp. 78–89; Sheldon D. Rose, *Group Treatment of Children—A Behavioral Approach* (San Francisco, Jossey-Bass, 1972).

17. Richard B. Stuart, "Operant-Interpersonal Treatment for Marital Discord," in Tony Tripodi et al., *Social Workers at Work,* pp. 32–41.

18. Jack Rothman, "Community Organization Practice," in Henry S. Maas, *Research in the Social Services*, pp. 70–107.

19. William Schwartz, pp. 167–92; and Scott Briar, "Family Services and Casework" in Henry S. Maas, *Research in the Social Services*, pp. 108–29.

20. Scott Briar, "Family Services and Casework," p. 111 and Scott Briar, "Family Services," in Henry S. Maas, *Five Fields of Social Service*, p. 13.

21. J. Michael Brittain, *Information and Its Users* (New York, Wiley Interscience, 1970), p. 104.

22. J. W. McCulloch and M. J. Brown, "What do Social Workers Read?" *New Society*, No. 316 (October 17, 1968), p. 560.

23. Aaron Rosenblatt, "The Practitioner's Use and Evaluation of Research," *Social Work*, 13 (January 1968), 53–59.

24. Joseph W. Eaton, "Symbolic and Substantive Evaluative Research," in Herbert C. Schulberg, Alan Sheldon, and Frank Baker, eds., *Program Evaluation in the Health Fields* (New York, Behavioral Publications, 1969), p. 507.

25. *Ibid.*, p. 515.

26. Henry S. Maas, ed., *Research in the Social Services.*

27. Tony Tripodi, Phillip Fellin, and Henry J. Meyer, *The Assessment of Social Research* (Itasca, Ill., F. E. Peacock, 1969), present guidelines for evaluating and utilizing research by means of reading research articles. This book incorporates, modifies, and extends some of those criteria in portions of chapters 2 and 3. Significant work on developing models of utilization are also contained in the following references: Edwin J. Thomas, ed., *Behavioral Science for Social Workers* (New York, Free Fress, 1967); Report on a Conference, *Building Social Work Knowledge* (New York, National Association of Social Workers, 1964); Henry J. Meyer, Eugene Litwak, Edwin J. Thomas, and Robert D. Vinter, "Social Work and Social Welfare," in Paul F. Lazarsfeld, William H. Sewell, and Harold L. Wilensky, eds., *The Uses of Sociology* (New York, Basic Books, 1967); Alvin W. Gouldner and S. M. Miller, eds., *Applied Sociology: Opportunities and Problems* (New York, Free Press, 1965); Herbert C. Schulberg, Alan Sheldon, and Frank Baker, eds., *Program Evaluation in the Health Fields* (New York, Behavioral Publications, 1969); Ronald G. Havelock, *Planning for Innovation through Dissemination and Utilization of Knowledge* (Ann Arbor, University of Michigan, Institute for Social Research, 1971); and Douglas C. McDonald, *Some Problems in the Organization and Use of Social Research in the U.S. Navy* (New York, Columbia University, Bureau of Applied Social Research, 1972).

28. See the following texts which describe the conduct of social research: Claire Selltiz, Marie Jahoda, Morton Deutsch, and Stuart W. Cook, *Research Methods in Social Relations* (rev. ed.; New York, Holt, Rinehart and Winston, 1959); David S. Dustin, *How Psychologists Do Research* (Englewood Cliffs, N.J., Prentice-Hall, 1969); Dennis P. Forcese and Stephen Richer, eds., *Stages of Social Research* (Englewood Cliffs, N.J., Prentice-Hall, 1970); John W. Best, *Research in Education* (2d ed.; Englewood Cliffs, N.J., Prentice-Hall, 1970); Harris K. Goldstein, *Research Standards and Methods for Social Workers* (New Orleans, Hauser Press, 1963); and Sanford Labovitz and Robert Hagedorn, *Introduction to Social Research* (New York, McGraw-Hill, 1971).

29. Arthur J. Bachrach, *Psychological Research* (2d ed.; New York, Random House, 1965), p. ix.

30. In addition, this example of the research process is also derived from Ted B. Palmer, "California Community Treatment Program for Delinquency Adolescents," *Journal of Research in Crime and Delinquency*, 8 (January 1971), 74–92. Other illustrations of the process of research are in Arthur J. Vidich, Joseph Bensman, and Maurice R. Stein, eds., *Reflections on Community Studies* (New York, Harper and Row, 1964), and Claire Selltiz et al., pp. 9–23.

202   1. Social Research and Social Work

31. For other definitions of social research, see Sidney E. Zimbalist," Major Trends in Social Work Research: An Analysis of the Nature and Development of Research in Social Work, as Seen in the Periodical Literature, 1900–1950," unpublished doctoral dissertation, George Warren Brown School of Social Work, Washington University, 1955, p. 12; Ernest Greenwood, "Social Work Research: A Decade of Reappraisal," *Social Service Review*, 31 (September 1957), 312; John W. Best, pp. 8–15; and Tony Tripodi et al., *The Assessment of Social Research*, p. 2.

32. Some texts also include the strategy of historical research. For example, see John W. Best, pp. 94–115. However, most texts on research primarily deal with experimentation, survey, and the case study. In this regard, see Dennis P. Forcese and Stephen Richer; and Sanford Labovitz and Robert Hagedorn, *Introduction to Social Research* (New York, McGraw-Hill, 1971), pp. 41–48.

33. Sanford Labovitz and Robert Hagedorn, pp. 1–11.

34. David S. Dustin, pp. 2–9.

35. John W. Best, pp. 144–46.

36. Alfred J. Kahn, "The Design of Research," in Norman A. Polansky ed., *Social Work Research* (Chicago, University of Chicago Press, 1960), pp. 48–73, and Edward S. Suchman, *Evaluative Research* (New York, Russell Sage Foundation, 1967), pp. 91–114.

37. See Robert Plutchik, *Foundations of Experimental Research* (New York, Harper and Row, 1968), pp. 171–203, and Allen L. Edwards, *Experimental Design in Psychological Research* (rev. ed.; New York, Holt, Rinehart and Winston, 1960), pp. 158–223.

38. For a summary of sources of contamination in experiments and the relative advantages and disadvantages of a variety of quasi-experiments, see Donald T. Campbell and Julian C. Stanley, *Experimental and Quasi-Experimental Designs for Research* (Chicago, Rand McNally, 1966).

39. Herbert Hyman, *Survey Design and Analysis* (Glencoe, Ill., Free Press, 1957), pp. 66–89.

40. See C. A. Moser, *Survey Methods in Social Investigation* (London, Heinemann, 1965), pp. 56–161, for a detailed discussion of sampling principles and procedures used in surveys.

41. Charles Y. Glock, "Survey Design and Analysis in Sociology," in Charles Y. Glock, ed., *Survey Research in the Social Sciences* (New York, Russell Sage Foundation, 1967), p. 42.

42. *Ibid.*, pp. 50–57.

43. Sanford Labovitz and Robert Hagedorn, p. 42.

44. Charles Y. Glock, pp. 42–56; Sanford Labovitz and Robert Hagedorn, p. 42.

45. For a number of detailed examples of case studies, see David S. Dustin, pp. 10–16; William J. Filstead, ed., *Qualitative Methodology* (Chicago, Markham, 1970); and Arthur J. Vidich et al.

46. Matilda W. Riley, *Sociological Research* (New York, Harcourt, Brace and World, 1963), pp. 502–69.

47. For a detailed description of this procedure, see Barney G. Glaser and Anselm L. Strauss, "Discovery of Substantive Theory: A Basic Strategy Underlying Qualitative Research," in William J. Filstead, pp. 288–304.

48. Sanford Labovitz and Robert Hagedorn, pp. 41–42.

49. Tony Tripodi et al., *Social Program Evaluation,* pp. 91–93.

50. This classification is derived from Sanford Labovitz and Robert Hagedorn, pp. 50–63; and from Claire Selltiz et al., pp. 199–304. Most of the ideas presented under observational techniques are discussed in the above references.

51. For a discussion of questionnaire construction, see C. A. Moser, pp. 175–84 and 210–45.

52. See Robert L. Kahn and Charles F. Cannell, *The Dynamics of Interviewing* (New York, Wiley, 1965), for a comprehensive discussion of interviewing techniques.

53. A wide range of tests and issues related to their construction and use is presented in Anne Anastasi, *Psychological Testing* (3d ed.; New York, Macmillan, 1968).

54. Henry S. Maas and Norman A. Polansky, "Collecting Original Data" in Norman A. Polansky, pp. 125–54.

55. Participant observation is regarded by some investigators as the major technique for securing qualitative data. A comprehensive view of the problems, issues, and use of this technique is contained in William J. Filstead, and George J. McCall and J. L. Simmons, eds., *Issues in Participant Observation* (Reading, Mass., Addison-Wesley, 1969).

56. Claire Selltiz et al., p. 345.

57. This scale is one of the scales developed by Robert B. Ellsworth, *Manual: The MACC Behavioral Adjustment Scale (Form II)* (Beverly Hills, Western Psychological Services, 1962).

58. For ways in which researchers attempt to solve these problems, see Fred B. Kerlinger, *Foundations of Behavioral Research* (New York, Holt, Rinehart and Winston, 1967), pp. 479–524.

59. Sanford Labovitz and Robert Hagedorn, pp. 50–51.

60. Herbert Hyman, p. 67.

61. Matilda W. Riley, pp. 194–255, and Fred B. Kerlinger, pp. 539–53.

62. Claire Selltiz et al., pp. 316–23.

63. *Ibid.,* pp. 255–68.

64. Fred B. Kerlinger, pp. 419–28; Claire Selltiz et al., pp. 186–98.

65. For detailed discussions of the relationship of levels of measurement to statistical operations, see W. Torgerson, *Theory and Methods of Scaling* (New York,

Wiley, 1958), and Hubert M. Blalock, *Social Statistics* (New York, McGraw-Hill, 1960).

66. Claire Selltiz et al., pp. 166–86.

67. An extensive discussion of the statistical theory of reliability and the use of correlational methods is contained in J. P. Guilford, *Fundamental Statistics for Psychology and Education* (4th ed.; New York, McGraw-Hill, 1965).

68. Marvin E. Shaw and Jack M. Wright, *Scales for the Measurement of Attitudes* (New York, McGraw-Hill, 1967), pp. 17–20.

69. In this chapter I have incorporated the concepts of concurrent validity and construct validity into the notion of predictive validity, for prediction is fundamental to all three types. For a discussion of validity, refer to Fred B. Kerlinger, pp. 442–62.

Chapter 2. Knowledge from Social Research

1. An extensive report of the problems in assembling social work knowledge is presented in Report of a Conference, *Building Social Work Knowledge* (New York, National Association of Social Workers, 1964).

2. Ernest Greenwood, "Social Work Research: A Decade of Reappraisal," *Social Service Review*, 31 (September 1957), 311–20.

3. Edwin J. Thomas, "Selecting Knowledge from Behavioral Science," in Edwin J. Thomas, ed., *Behavioral Science for Social Workers* (New York, Free Press, 1967), pp. 417–24.

4. *Ibid.*, p. 418; Charlotte Towle, "A Social Work Approach to Courses in Human Growth and Behavior," *Social Service Review*, 34 (December 1960), 402–15.

5. Edwin J. Thomas, p. 419.

6. Henry S. Maas, ed., *Five Fields of Social Service: Reviews of Research* (New York, National Association of Social Workers, 1966), p. 5.

7. Scott Briar, "Family Services," in Henry S. Maas, pp. 9–50.

8. This conception has also been employed by Ernest Greenwood, *Lectures in Research Methodology for Social Welfare Students*, University of California Syllabus Series No. 388 (Berkeley, University of California, 1960); Edwin J. Thomas, "Selecting Knowledge from Behavioral Science," in Report of a Conference, pp. 38–48; and Tony Tripodi, Phillip Fellin, and Henry J. Meyer, *The Assessment of Social Research* (Itasca, Ill., F. E. Peacock, 1969).

9. Lilian Ripple, "Problem Identification and Formulation," in Norman A. Polansky, ed., *Social Work Research* (Chicago, University of Chicago Press, 1960), pp. 41–44.

10. Hans L. Zetterberg, *On Theory and Verification in Sociology* (3d rev. ed.; Totowa, N.J., Bedminster Press, 1965; Ernest Greenwood, *Lectures in Research Methodology*; William J. Goode and Paul K. Hatt, *Methods in Social Research* (New York, McGraw-Hill, 1952); Lilian Ripple, pp. 41–44; and Sanford Labovitz

and Robert Hagedorn, *Introduction to Social Research* (New York, McGraw-Hill, 1971), pp. 19–22.

11. Lilian Ripple and Ernestina Alexander, "Motivation, Capacity, and Opportunity as Related to the Use of Casework Service: Nature of Client's Problem," in Phillip Fellin, Tony Tripodi, and Henry J. Meyer, eds., *Exemplars of Social Research* (Itasca, Ill., F. E. Peacock, 1969), p. 210.

12. Robert Presthus, "Community Power Structure: Theoretical Framework," in Fred M. Cox, John L. Erlich, Jack Rothman, and John E. Tropman, eds., *Strategies of Community Organization* (Itasca, Ill., F. E. Peacock, 1970), p. 104.

13. Sanford Labovitz and Robert Hagedorn, p. 18.

14. *Ibid.*, p. 25.

15. These types of hypotheses have been abstracted and devised from three basic sources: Lilian Ripple, pp. 37–41; Hans L. Zetterberg, pp. 63–100; and William J. Goode and Paul K. Hatt, pp. 59–63. Although there is overlap among descriptive, correlational, and cause-effect hypotheses, the typology is useful because it can direct our concerns to different types of knowledge which social research seeks to develop.

16. William J. Goode and Paul K. Hatt, p. 59.

17. Alfred Kadushin, "Child Welfare," in Henry S. Maas, ed., *Research in the Social Services: A Five Year Review* (New York, National Association of Social Workers, 1971), p. 46.

18. Bernard Berelson and Gary A. Steiner, *Human Behavior: An Inventory of Scientific Findings* (New York, Harcourt, Brace and World, 1964), p. 316.

19. Allan E. Bergin, "Implications of Psychotherapy Research," *International Journal of Psychiatry*, 3 (March 1967), 140.

20. *Ibid.*, p. 141.

21. Bernard Berelson and Gary A. Steiner, p. 365.

22. Scott Briar, p. 25.

23. Allan E. Bergin, p. 136.

24. Bernard Berelson and Gary A. Steiner, p. 141.

25. *Ibid.*, p. 329.

26. Ernest Greenwood, *Lectures in Research Methodology for Social Welfare Students*, ch. IV.

27. Clark L. Hull, *Principles of Behavior: An Introduction to Behavior Theory* (New York, Appleton-Century-Crofts, 1943), p. 382.

28. See Genevieve W. Carter, "Public Welfare," in Henry S. Maas, ed., *Research in the Social Services*, pp. 207–11.

29. Henry J. Meyer, Edgar F. Borgatta, and Wyatt C. Jones, *Girls at Vocational High: An Experiment in Social Work Intervention* (New York, Russell Sage Foundation, 1965); William J. Reid and Ann W. Shyne, *Brief and Extended Casework* (New York, Columbia University Press, 1969).

30. These criteria are abstracted and reorganized from the following sources: Tony Tripodi et al., *Assessment of Social Research*, pp. 60–93; David S. Dustin, *How Psychologists Do Research* (Englewood Cliffs, N.J., Prentice-Hall, 1969); Delbert C. Miller, *Handbook of Research Design and Social Measurement* (New York, David McKay, 1964); Donald T. Campbell and Julian C. Stanley, "Experimental and Quasi-Experimental Designs for Research in Teaching," in N. L. Gage, ed., *Handbook of Research on Teaching* (Chicago, Rand McNally, 1963), pp. 171–246; Harris K. Goldstein, *Research Standards and Methods for Social Workers* (New Orleans, Hauser Press, 1963); and William J. Filstead, ed., *Qualitative Methodology* (Chicago, Markham, 1970), pp. 52–62.

31. Lilian Ripple and Ernestina Alexander, p. 210.

32. Herbert Blumer, "What is Wrong with Social Theory," in William J. Filstead, pp. 52–62.

33. For an inventory of indicators related to social class, see Delbert C. Miller, pp. 97–122.

34. These criteria are modifications of those postulated by William J. Goode and Paul K. Hatt, pp. 68–73:
   "1. The hypotheses must be conceptually clear.
   2. Hypotheses must have empirical referents.
   3. The hypotheses must be specific.
   4. Hypotheses should be related to available techniques.
   5. The hypotheses should be related to a body of theory."

35. The criterion of accuracy of measurement has been used to evaluate research studies about anxiety; see David S. Dustin, pp. 3–4. In addition, the characteristics of measurement classification, reliability and validity have been employed to evaluate research studies in social science and social work; in this regard, see Tony Tripodi et al., *Assessment of Social Research*, pp. 60–93.

36. Henry S. Maas and Norman A. Polansky, "Collecting Original Data," in Norman A. Polansky, p. 137.

37. For a discussion of data processing principles and procedures, see C. A. Moser, *Survey Methods in Social Investigation* (London, Heinemann, 1965), pp. 269–87.

38. The criterion of empirical generality is abstracted from two basic sources: 1) from the notion of "external validity" as articulated by Donald T. Campbell, "Factors Relevant to the Validity of Experiments in Social Settings," in Herbert C. Schulberg, Alan Sheldon, and Frank Baker, eds., *Program Evaluation in the Health Fields* (New York, Behavioral Publications, 1969), pp. 165–86; 2) from the notion of "generalization" as employed by David S. Dustin, pp. 4–5.

39. Sanford Labovitz and Robert Hagedorn, pp. 28–35.

40. The criterion of internal control is a modification of the notion of "internal validity" as defined by Donald T. Campbell in Herbert C. Schulberg et al., pp. 165–85. Whereas internal validity includes criteria related to measurement accuracy, internal control does not.

3. Using the Results of Social Research   207

41. These questions are derived from Tony Tripodi et al., *Assessment of Social Research,* pp. 75–87.

42. Procedures employed for testing cause-effect hypotheses through experimentation are discussed in chapter 1. Furthermore, a detailed evaluation of an experimental study is provided in *ibid.,* pp. 135–65.

43. This scheme is a modification and extension of guidelines for evaluating research studies in *ibid.,* pp. 75–87.

Chapter 3. Using the Results of Social Research

1. These two types of knowledge are abstracted from the work of Edwin J. Thomas, "Types of Contributions Behavioral Science Makes to Social Work," in Edwin J. Thomas, ed., *Behavioral Science for Social Workers* (New York, Free Press, 1967), pp. 3–13. Thomas discusses four types of knowledge: scientific stance, conceptualization, substantive, and methods of research. In this book scientific stance and methods of research are regarded as methodological knowlege, while conceptualization is subsumed under substantive knowledge.

2. Reviews of this literature are available in two basic sources: Tony Tripodi, Phillip Fellin and Henry J. Meyer, *The Assessment of Social Research* (Itasca, Ill., F. E. Peacock, 1969), pp. 95–125; and J. M. Brittain, *Information and Its Users* (New York, Wiley Interscience, 1970), pp. 101–20.

3. The most thorough works in this regard are by Ronald G. Havelock, *Planning for Innovation Through Dissemination and Utilization of Knowledge* (Ann Arbor, University of Michigan, Center for Research on Utilization of Scientific Knowledge, Institute for Social Research, 1971); and J. M. Brittain, *Information and Its Users,* p. 4. This chapter is based on personal observations in teaching research utilization to social work students and in serving as an evaluation consultant to a number of social agencies, and on the following major references, already cited: Ronald G. Havelock; Tony Tripodi et al., *Assessment of Social Research;* J. M. Brittain; Edwin J. Thomas; and on Herbert C. Schulberg, Alan Sheldon, and Frank Baker, eds., *Program Evaluation in the Health Fields* (New York, Behavioral Publications, 1969); and Report on a Conference, *Building Social Work Knowledge* (New York, National Association of Social Workers, 1964).

4. Herbert Menzel, "Scientific Communication: Five Themes from Social Science Research," in Herbert C. Schulberg et al., pp. 487–89.

5. *Ibid.,* p. 489.

6. See *ibid.,* pp. 490–96, for a discussion of information principles and documentations regarding the role of formal and informal sources of communication.

7. Harold P. Halpert, "Communications as a Basic Tool in Promoting Utilization of Research Findings," in Herbert C. Schulberg et al., pp. 497–505; J. C. R. Licklider, "A Crux in Scientific and Technical Communication," *American Psychologist,* 21 (November 1966), 1044–51.

8. Leonard Kogan, "The Utilization of Social Work Research," *Social Casework*, 44 (December 1963), pp. 569–74.

9. Ronald G. Havelock, ch. 11, pp. 1–44.

10. David Fanshel, ed., *Research in Social Welfare Administration* (New York, National Association of Social Workers, 1962), pp. 121–25.

11. Leonard Kogan, pp. 569–74.

12. Alfred Kadushin, "Child Welfare," in Henry S. Maas, ed., *Research in the Social Services: A Five Year Review* (New York, National Association of Social Workers, 1971), pp. 33–51.

13. Content relevance is a criterion employed for selecting knowledge by Edwin J. Thomas, "Selecting Knowledge from Behavioral Science" in Report of a Conference, pp. 39–42. His conception of relevant content relates to subject matter and levels to which subject matter are applied. The conception of content relevance that is used in this book, although derived from Thomas' notion, refers more directly to the tasks and functions of practicing social workers. It is to be further noted that, as was pointed out in chapter 2, the concept of "content relevance" is not as useful for facilitating communications between researchers and social workers as is the notion of knowledge levels.

14. This definition is derived from Edwin J. Thomas, pp. 43–45, and J. M. Brittain, pp. 52–53. The discussion of accessibility of knowledge in this chapter is based upon and stimulated by these references, as well as the works of Alvin W. Gouldner, "Theoretical Requirements of the Applied Social Sciences," *American Sociological Review*, 22 (February 1957), 92–103; and Tony Tripodi et al., *Assessment of Social Research*, pp. 119–21.

15. The notions of identifiability and manipulability have been employed by Edwin J. Thomas, *Behavioral Science for Social Workers*, pp. 43–45, and the concept of engineerability is described in Tony Tripodi et al., *Assessment of Social Research*, pp. 119–21.

16. See Robert C. Day and Robert L. Hamblin, "Some Effects of Close and Punitive Styles of Supervision," in Phillip Fellin, Tony Tripodi, and Henry J. Meyer, eds., *Exemplars of Social Research* (Itasca, Ill., F. E. Peacock, 1969), pp. 32–47.

17. David B. Guralnik, ed., *Webster's New World Dictionary: Second College Edition* (New York, World, 1970), p. 49.

18. For a detailed example of practice principles derived by analogies from small group psychology and learning theory, see Sheldon D. Rose, "A Behavioral Approach to the Group Treatment of Parents," in Tony Tripodi, Phillip Fellin, Irwin Epstein, and Roger Lind, eds., *Social Workers at Work: An Introduction to Social Work Practice* (Itasca, Ill., F. E. Peacock, 1972), pp. 78–89.

19. Discussions of knowledge receptivity are derived from and stimulated by the work of Ronald G. Havelock, ch. 11, pp. 20–25.

20. See John M. Shlien, "Comparison of Results with Different Forms of Psychotherapy," in Gary E. Stollak, Bernard G. Guerney, Jr., and Meyer Rothberg, eds., *Psychotherapy Research* (Chicago, Rand McNally, 1966), pp. 156–62; and Carl R.

Rogers and Rosalind F. Dymond, eds., *Psychotherapy and Personality Change* (Chicago, University of Chicago Press, 1954).

21. Examples of converting research knowledge from social science to social work are contained in these references: Edwin J. Thomas, *Behavioral Science for Social Workers;* Tony Tripodi et al., *Assessment of Social Research,* pp. 99–105; Henry J. Meyer, Eugene Litwak, Edwin J. Thomas, and Robert D. Vinter, "Social Work and Social Welfare," in Paul F. Lazarsfeld, William H. Sewell, and Harold L. Wilensky, eds., *The Uses of Sociology* (New York, Basic Books, 1967), pp. 156–90; Jack Rothman, "Community Organization Practice," in Henry S. Maas, ed., *Research in the Social Services,* pp. 70–107.

22. Carl J. Hovland, Irving L. Janis, and Harold H. Kelley, *Communications and Persuasion: Psychological Studies of Opinion Change* (New Haven, Yale University Press, 1953).

23. Edward A. Suchman, *Evaluative Research* (New York, Russell Sage Foundation, 1967), p. 33.

24. Robert F. Boruch, "Maintaining Confidentiality of Data in Educational Research: A Systematic Analysis," *American Psychologist,* 26 (May 1971), 413–30.

25. For a compilation of articles pertaining to the role of ethics in social research, see Gideon Sjoberg, ed., *Ethics, Politics and Social Research* (Cambridge, Schenkman, 1967).

26. See Arthur G. Miller, "Role Playing: An Alternative to Deception?" *American Psychologist,* 27 (July 1972), 623–36, for a discussion of different viewpoints on the issue of using deception in experimentation with human subjects.

27. This criterion is derived from the work of Ronald G. Havelock, ch. 11, pp. 1–44, who uses the dimensions of linkage, structure, openness, capacity, reward, proximity, and synergy for discussing the utilization of scientific knowledge. Other works which influenced the discussion of implementation capability are as follows: Harold P. Halpert, in Herbert C. Schulberg, pp. 497–505; Herbert Hyman, *Survey Design and Analysis* (Glencoe, Ill., Free Press, 1955), pp. 344–63; Rensis Likert and Ronald Lippitt, "The Utilization of Social Science," in Leon Festinger and Daniel Katz, eds., *Research Methods in the Behavioral Sciences* (New York, Dryden Press, 1953), pp. 581–646; and Report of a Conference.

28. See Edwin J. Thomas, Robert D. Carter, and Eileen D. Gambrill, "Some Possibilities of Behavioral Modification of Marital Problems Using 'SAM' (Signal System for the Assessment and Modification of Behavior), in R. D. Rubin, H. Fernsterheim, A. A. Lazarus, and C. M. Franks, eds., *Advances in Behavior Therapy* (New York, Academic Press, 1971), pp. 273–87.

Chapter 4. Using Social Research Methods

1. Edwin J. Thomas, "Types of Contributions Behavioral Science Makes to Social Work," in Edwin J. Thomas, ed., *Behavioral Science for Social Workers* (New York, Free Press, 1967), pp. 8–9.

2. Harris K. Goldstein, "Making Practice More Scientific Through Knowledge of Research," *Social Work*, 7 (July 1962), 108–12; Tony Tripodi, Phillip Fellin, and Henry J. Meyer, *The Assessment of Social Research* (Itasca, Ill., F. E. Peacock, 1969), p. 117.

3. See ch. 4, "Techniques of Evaluation," in Tony Tripodi, Phillip Fellin, and Irwin Epstein, *Social Program Evaluation: Guidelines for Health, Education and Welfare Administrators* (Itasca, Ill., F. E. Peacock, 1971), pp. 61–111.

4. Robert Morris, "Social Planning," in Henry S. Maas, ed., *Five Fields of Social Service: Reviews of Research* (New York, National Association of Social Workers, 1966), pp. 185–208.

5. A comprehensive review of the development and application of techniques used in behavior therapy is provided by Aubrey J. Yates, *Behavior Therapy* (New York, Wiley, 1970).

6. Leon Festinger and Daniel Katz, eds., *Research Methods in the Behavioral Sciences* (New York, Dryden Press, 1953); Herbert Hyman, *Survey Design and Analysis* (Glencoe, Ill., Free Press, 1955); C. A. Moser, *Survey Methods in Social Investigation* (London, Heinemann, 1958); Claire Selltiz, Marie Jahoda, Morton Deutsch, and Stuart W. Cook, *Research Methods in Social Relations* (New York, Holt, Rinehart and Winston, 1959); Fred N. Kerlinger, *Foundations of Behavioral Research* (New York, Holt, Rinehart and Winston, 1964); William J. Filstead, ed., *Qualitative Methodology* (Chicago, Markham, 1970); Victor H. Vroom ed., *Methods of Organizational Research* (Pittsburgh, University of Pittsburgh Press, 1967).

7. Gary E. Stollak, Bernard G. Guerney, Jr., and Meyer Rothberg, eds., *Psychotherapy Research* (Chicago, Rand McNally, 1966); Arnold P. Goldstein and Sanford J. Dean, eds., *The Investigation of Psychotherapy* (New York, Wiley, 1966); Carol H. Weiss, *Evaluation Research* (Englewood Cliffs, N.J., Prentice-Hall, 1972); Leonard Krasner and Leonard P. Ullmann, eds., *Research in Behavior Modification* (New York, Holt, Rinehart and Winston, 1965); Howard E. Freeman and Clarence C. Sherwood, *Social Research and Public Policy* (Englewood Cliffs, N.J., Prentice-Hall, 1970); Tony Tripodi et al., *Social Program Evaluation;* Arthur J. Vidich, Joseph Bensman, and Maurice R. Stein, eds., *Reflections on Community Studies* (New York, Harper and Row, 1971); Travis Hirschi and Hanan C. Selvin, *Delinquency Research* (New York, Free Press, 1967).

8. Robert L. Kahn and Charles F. Cannell, *The Dynamics of Interviewing* (New York, Wiley, 1957); Stanley L. Payne, *The Art of Asking Questions* (Princeton, Princeton University Press, 1951); Frederick J. Stephen and Philip J. McCarthy, *Sampling Opinions* (New York, Wiley, 1963); Allen L. Edwards, *Experimental Design in Psychological Research* (rev. ed.; New York, Holt, Rinehart and Winston, 1960); Seymour Sudman, *Reducing the Cost of Surveys* (Chicago, Aldine, 1967); Walter Mischel, *Personality and Assessment* (New York, Wiley, 1968); George J. McCall and J. L. Simmons, eds., *Issues in Participant Observation* (Reading, Mass., Addison-Wesley, 1969).

9. Marvin E. Shaw and Jack M. Wright, eds., *Scales for the Measurement of Attitudes* (New York, McGraw-Hill, 1967); Samuel B. Lyerly and Preston S. Abbott,

eds., *Handbook of Psychiatric Rating Scales* (1950–1964) (Bethesda, Md., National Institute of Mental Health, Public Health Service Publication No. 1495, 1965); Stephen Isaac, in collaboration with William B. Michael, *Handbook in Research and Evaluation* (San Diego, Robert R. Knapp, 1971); Delbert C. Miller, *Handbook of Research Design and Social Measurement* (New York, David McKay, 1964); Oscar K. Buros, ed., *The Sixth Mental Measurements Yearbook* (Highland Park, N.J., Gryphon Press, 1965).

10. Fremont J. Lyden and Ernest G. Miller, eds., *A Systems Approach to Management* (Chicago, Markham, 1968).

11. Carl R. Rogers and Rosalind F. Dymond, eds., *Psychotherapy and Personality Change* (Chicago, University of Chicago Press, 1954).

12. Leonard S. Kogan, J. McVicker Hunt, and Phyllis F. Bartelme, *A Follow-up Study of the Results of Social Casework* (New York, Family Service Association of America, 1953); Ludwig L. Geismar and Beverly Ayres, *Measuring Family Functioning* (St. Paul, Greater St. Paul United Fund and Council, 1960).

13. William J. Reid and Ann W. Shyne, *Brief and Extended Casework* (New York, Columbia University Press, 1969), pp. 55–95; Lilian Ripple and Ernestina Alexander, "Motivation, Capacity, and Opportunity as Related to the Use of Casework Service: Nature of Client's Problem," in Phillip Fellin, Tony Tripodi, and Henry J. Meyer, eds., *Exemplars of Social Research* (Itasca, Ill., F. E. Peacock, 1969), pp. 204–24.

14. Arthur W. Staats and Carolyn K. Staats, *Complex Human Behavior* (New York, Holt, Rinehart and Winston, 1963).

15. Sheldon D. Rose, *Group Treatment of Children: A Behavioral Approach* (San Francisco, Jossey-Bass, 1972).

16. William B. McCurdy, "An Approach to the Co-ordination of Statistical Reporting by Voluntary Agencies," *Social Casework*, 44 (April 1963), 193–99.

17. Richard A. Cloward and Irwin Epstein, "Private Social Welfare's Disengagement from the Poor: The Case of Family Adjustment Agencies," in Mayer N. Zald, ed., *Social Welfare Institutions* (New York, Wiley, 1965), pp. 623–44.

18. For discussions pertaining to the use of telephones in interviewing, as well as other techniques for gathering information quickly and cheaply, see Seymour Sudman, *Reducing the Cost of Surveys.*

19. An introduction to techniques of evaluation is provided in Tony Tripodi et al., *Social Program Evaluation*, pp. 61–109.

20. These procedures are employed in the research strategy of case studies, see *ibid.*, pp. 91–95.

21. For a detailed presentation of the planning of social experiments, see George A. Fairweather, *Methods for Experimental Social Innovation* (New York, Wiley, 1967).

22. Arthur G. Miller, "Role Playing: An Alternative to Deception?" *American Psychologist*, 27 (July 1972), 623–36.

23. Robert F. Bales, *Interaction Process Analysis* (Reading, Mass., Addison-Wesley, 1950).

24. Tony Tripodi et al., *Social Program Evaluation,* pp. 117–18.

25. See Helen H. Perlman, *Social Casework: A Problem Solving Process* (Chicago, University of Chicago Press, 1957); Florence Hollis, *Casework: A Psychosocial Therapy* (2d ed.; New York, Random House, 1972); Scott Briar and Henry Miller, *Problems and Issues in Social Casework* (New York, Columbia University Press, 1971); Robert D. Vinter, ed., *Readings in Group Work Practice* (Ann Arbor, Campus Publishers, 1967); Alfred J. Kahn, *Theory and Practice of Social Planning* (New York, Russell Sage Foundation, 1969); Fred M. Cox, John L. Erlich, Jack Rothman, and John E. Tropman, eds., *Strategies of Community Organization* (Itasca, Ill., F. E. Peacock, 1971); Robert Morris and Robert H. Binstock, with Martin Rein, *Feasible Planning for Social Change* (New York, Columbia University Press, 1966); and Harry A. Schatz, ed., *Social Work Administration: A Resource Book* (New York, Council on Social Work Education, 1970).

26. These components were derived and adapted from Charles D. Garvin and Paul H. Glasser, "Social Group Work: The Preventive and Rehabilitative Approach," *Encyclopedia of Social Work* (New York, National Association of Social Workers, 1971), II, 1263–73; and from Tony Tripodi, Phillip Fellin, Irwin Epstein, and Roger Lind., eds., *Social Workers at Work: An Introduction to Social Work Practice* (Itasca, Ill., F. E. Peacock, 1972), pp. 1–10 and 109–16.

27. For an indication of the range of the functions and tasks of social workers, see Tony Tripodi et al., *Social Workers at Work.*

28. See chapter 1 in this book, where the process of social research is described in detail.

29. The discussion of the practice-research analogy is primarily derived from and stimulated by these works: Harris K. Goldstein, "Making Practice More Scientific Through Knowledge of Research," *Social Work,* 7 (July 1962), 108–12; Harris K. Goldstein, *Research Standards and Methods for Social Workers* (New Orleans, Hauser Press, 1963); and Scott Briar and Henry Miller, ch. 4, "The Scientific Method in Casework Practice," pp. 79–88.

30. Delbert C. Miller, pp. 273–93.

31. See Frederick H. Kanfer and George Saslow, "Behavior Diagnosis," in Cyril M. Franks, ed., *Behavior Therapy: Appraisal and Status* (New York, McGraw-Hill, 1969), pp. 417–44; Roland G. Tharp and Ralph J. Wetzel, *Behavior and Modification in the Natural Environment* (New York, Academic Press, 1969).

32. For a comprehensive review of available psychological tests and for considerations of their uses, see Anne Anastasi, *Psychological Testing* (3d ed.; New York, Macmillan, 1968).

33. Samuel B. Lyerly and Preston S. Abbott, *Handbook of Psychiatric Rating Scales (1950–1964).*

34. Marvin E. Shaw and Jack M. Wright, eds., *Scales for the Measurement of Attitudes* (New York, McGraw-Hill, 1967).

35. Marvin E. Shaw and Jack M. Wright, pp. 33–68, 415–27.

36. George A. Kelly, *The Psychology of Personal Constructs*, Vol. 1 (New York, Norton, 1955); James Bieri, Alvin L. Atkins, Scott Briar, Robin L. Leaman, Henry Miller, and Tony Tripodi, *Clinical and Social Judgement* (New York, Wiley, 1966), pp. 189–93.

37. Seymour Sudman, *Reducing the Cost of Surveys;* Herbert Hyman, *Survey Design and Analysis.*

38. U.S. Department of Health, Education and Welfare, *Toward A Social Report* (Ann Arbor, University of Michigan Press, 1970).

39. Ernest Greenwood, "Social Work Research: A Decade of Reappraisal," *Social Service Review,* 31 (September 1957), 311–20.

40. Theodore B. Palmer and Marguerite Q. Warren, *Community Treatment Project Report No. 8* (Sacramento, State of California, Department of Youth Authority, 1967); Otto F. Kernberg, Esther D. Burstein, Lolafaye Coyne, Ann Appelbaum, Leonard Horwitz, and Harold Voth, "Psychotherapy and Psychoanalysis," *Bulletin of the Menninger Clinic,* 36 (January–March 1972), 1–275.

41. See Gerald Marsden, "Content-Analysis Studies of Therapeutic Interviews: 1954 to 1964," in Gary E. Stollak, Bernard G. Guerney, Jr., and Meyer Rothberg, *Psychotherapy Research,* pp. 336–64.

42. George A. Talland and David H. Clark, "Evaluation of Topics in Therapy Group Discussion," in Gary E. Stollak, Bernard G. Guerney, Jr., and Meyer Rothberg, *Psychotherapy Research,* pp. 365–71.

43. Tony Tripodi et al., *Social Program Evaluation,* pp. 25–60.

Chapter 5. Abusing Social Research

1. A detailed consideration of abuses that occur in the giving and receiving of research funds is available in Harold Orlans, "Ethical Problems in the Relations of Research Sponsors and Investigators," in Gideon Sjoberg, ed., *Ethics, Politics, and Social Research* (Cambridge, Schenkman, 1967), pp. 3–24.

2. Frank von Hippel and Joel Primack, "Public Interest Science," *Science,* 177 (September 1972), 1166–71; Kurt Lang, "Pitfalls and Politics in Commissioned Policy Research," in Irving L. Horowitz, ed., *The Use and Abuse of Social Science* (New Brunswick, N.J., Transaction Books, 1971), pp. 212–33.

3. This example is based on the author's personal observations in meetings between a neighborhood organization, city officials, and the chief of police in a Canadian city.

4. See Irving Horowitz, *Use and Abuse of Social Science,* for a series of articles pertaining to the relationship of social science and national policy.

5. Kurt Lang, in Horowitz, p. 219.

6. See Tony Tripodi, Phillip Fellin, and Irwin Epstein, *Social Program Evalua-*

tion: Guidelines for Administrators of Health, Education and Welfare Programs (Itasca, Ill., F. E. Peacock, 1971), pp. 3–23.

7. "A Matter of Morality," *Time* (August 7, 1972), p. 54.

8. See Arthur G. Miller, "Role Playing: An Alternative to Deception? A Review of the Evidence," *American Psychologist,* 27 (July 1972), 623–36; Robert F. Boruch, "Maintaining Confidentiality of Data in Educational Research: A Systematic Analysis," *American Psychologist,* 26 (May 1971), 413–30; Arthur G. Nikelly, "Ethical Issues in Research on Student Protest," *American Psychologist,* 26 (May 1971), 475–78; and Gideon Sjoberg, ed., *Ethics, Politics and Social Research.*

9. Tony Tripodi, Phillip Fellin, and Henry J. Meyer, *The Assessment of Social Research* (Itasca, Ill., F. E. Peacock, 1969), pp. 69–70.

10. Leonard D. Cain, Jr., "The AMA and the Gerontologists: Uses and Abuses of 'A Profile of the Aging: U.S.A.'," in Gideon Sjoberg, pp. 78–114.

11. Travis Hirschi and Hanan C. Selvin, *Delinquency Research: An Appraisal of Analytic Methods* (New York, Free Press, 1967), pp. 258–69. This study provides an excellent analysis of the kinds of errors that take place in the interpretation of data from surveys.

12. *Ibid.*

13. In this regard, Travis Hirschi and Hanan C. Selvin, pp. 145–74, provide a discussion of techniques employed in multivariate analysis.

14. A number of statistical abuses have been identified in the literature on statistics and research, and the reader is referred to such exemplary sources as: W. Allen Wallis and Harry V. Roberts, *The Nature of Statistics* (New York, Free Press, 1962), pp. 89–122; Sanford I. Labovitz "Methods for Control with Small Sample Size," in Dennis P. Forcese and Stephen Richer, eds., *Stages of Social Research: Contemporary Perspectives* (Englewood Cliffs, N.J., Prentice-Hall, 1970), pp. 273–82; Sanford I. Labovitz, "Criteria for Selecting a Significance Level: A Note on the Sacredness of .05," in Dennis P. Forcese and Stephen Richer, pp. 322–25; and Leslie Kish, "Some Statistical Problems in Research Design," in Dennis P. Forcese and Stephen Richer, pp. 103–15.

15. See Allen L. Edwards, *Statistical Methods for the Behavioral Sciences* (New York, Holt, Rinehart and Winston, 1961), pp. 9–10, 300–14, for discussions of statistical inference pertaining to correlation.

16. *Ibid.*, pp. 246–77, 315–39, and 366–98.

17. An example of a research study which inappropriately uses statistical tests of significance is discussed in Tony Tripodi et al. *Assessment of Social Research,* pp. 183–95, and 203–7.

18. Leslie Kish, in Dennis P. Forcese and Stephen Richer, pp. 112–13.

19. For technical discussions of one- and two-tailed hypothesis testing, see Sidney Siegel, *Nonparametric Statistics for the Behavioral Sciences* (New York, McGraw-Hill, 1956), pp. 6–17; and Robert S. Weiss, *Statistics in Social Research* (New York, Wiley, 1968), pp. 244–54.

20. The numbers are taken from a table of t values in Hubert M. Blalock, *Social Statistics* (New York, McGraw-Hill, 1960), p. 442.

21. *Ibid.*, pp. 169–86.

22. Leslie Kish, pp. 113–14.

23. W. Allen Wallis and Harry V. Roberts, *The Nature of Statistics* (New York, Free Press, 1962), pp. 113–16.

24. *Ibid.*, pp. 45–140.

25. Leslie Kish, in Dennis P. Forcese and Stephen Richer, pp. 103–4.

26. Travis Hirschi and Hanan C. Selvin, p. 117.

27. *Ibid.*, p. 133.

28. Travis Hirschi and Hanan C. Selvin, pp. 114–41, have specified other false criteria of causality, and they indicate how those errors contribute to inappropriate inferences based on research in juvenile delinquency.

29. Edward A. Suchman, *Evaluative Research* (New York, Russell Sage Foundation, 1967), p. 143, defined the concept of "eye-wash" as "an attempt to justify a weak or bad program by deliberately selecting only those aspects that 'look good.' " The concept is broadened in this chapter to refer to individuals as well as to programs, and to include the possibility of undermining the performances of individuals and/or programs by deliberately attending only to those features that "look bad."

30. *Ibid.*, p. 43.

31. The concept of "hog-wash" is derived from the notion of "posture" as defined by Edward A. Suchman, p. 43: "Posture—an attempt to use evaluation as a 'gesture' of objectivity and to assume the pose of 'scientific' research."

Chapter 6. Facilitating Research Utilization

1. Henry S. Maas, "Introduction," in Henry S. Maas, ed., *Research in the Social Sciences: A Five Year Review* (New York, National Association of Social Workers, 1971), pp. 8–9; Carol H. Weiss, *Evaluation of Research: Methods of Assessing Program Effectiveness* (Englewood Cliffs, N.J., Prentice-Hall, 1972), pp. 110–28.

2. See George W. Fairweather, *Methods for Experimental Social Innovation* (New York, Wiley, 1967), pp. 20–36, for an extensive definition of experimental social innovation. In addition, the notion of "intentional experiments," which is analogous to that of experimental social innovation, is discussed by Glen C. Cain and Robinson G. Hollister, "The Methodology of Evaluating Social Action Programs," in Peter H. Rossi and Walter Williams, eds., *Evaluating Social Programs* (New York, Seminar Press, 1972), pp. 132–35.

3. For a discussion of issues and problems in the conduct of social experiments see David N. Kershaw, "Issues in Income Maintenance Experimentation," in Peter H. Rossi and Walter Williams, *Evaluating Social Programs,* pp. 221–45; and Carol H. Weiss, pp. 60–109.

4. Patricia R. Crawford, "Gary Income Maintenance Experiment (G-X)" (Gary,
Indiana University Northwest, Spring 1971), pp. 1–5.

5. Irving L. Horowitz, ed., *The Use and Abuse of Social Science* (New Brunswick, N.J., Transaction Books, 1971).

6. For other uses of surveys, see Fred Massarik, "The Survey Method in Social
Work: Past, Present, and Potential," in Charles Y. Glock, ed., *Survey Research in
the Social Sciences* (New York, Russell Sage Foundation, 1967), pp. 377–422.

7. *Ibid.,* pp. 388–92; Genevieve W. Carter, "Measurement of Need," in Norman
A. Polansky, ed., *Social Work Research* (Chicago, University of Chicago Press,
1960), pp. 201–22.

8. For examples of service utilization surveys, see Genevieve W. Carter, "Public
Welfare," in Henry S. Maas, ed., *Research in the Social Services: A Five Year
Review* (New York, National Association of Social Workers, 1971), pp. 207–8.

9. Tony Tripodi, Phillip Fellin, and Irwin Epstein, *Social Program Evaluation:
Guidelines for Administrators of Health, Education, and Welfare Programs*
(Itasca, Ill., F. E. Peacock, 1971), pp. 85–90.

10. The use of such designs leads to information that is less precise than that obtained from social experiments. However, the needs of social planners may
require that they obtain estimates of program effectiveness in short periods of
time, and evaluation surveys are often suitable. For a discussion of problems in
utilizing the results of an evaluation survey, see Walter Williams and John W.
Evans, "The Politics of Evaluation: The Case of Head Start," *Annals of the
American Academy of Political and Social Science,* 385 (September 1969),
118–32.

11. Richard T. Smith and Abraham M. Lilienfield, *The Social Security Disability
Program: An Evaluation Study* (Washington, D.C., U.S. Department of Health,
Education, and Welfare, Social Security Administration, Research Report No. 39,
June 1971), p. 2.

12. Richard B. Stuart, "Contingency Contracting with Predelinquent Youth,"
Application for Research Grant to National Institutes of Mental Health, Behavioral Change Laboratories, Ann Arbor, Michigan, 1970.

13. Richard B. Stuart and Tony Tripodi, "Experimental Evaluation of Three
Time-Constrained Behavioral Treatments for Predelinquents and Delinquents,"
in R. Rubin, ed., *Advances in Behavior Therapy* (New York, Academic Press, in
press).

14. Ronald G. Havelock, *Planning for Innovation Through Dissemination and
Utilization of Knowledge* (Ann Arbor, University of Michigan, Center for Research on Utilization of Scientific Knowledge, Institute for Social Research,
1971), ch. 10, pp. 1–89.

15. Jack Rothman, "Community Organization Practice," in Henry S. Maas,
Research in the Social Services, pp. 70–107; Jack Rothman and Project Staff,
*Guidelines for Social Change: Utilization of Social Science Research in Social
Planning and Community Action* (interim draft) (Ann Arbor, University of Mich-
igan, 1972).

16. Jack Rothman and Project Staff, ch. 1, pp. 12–13.

17. *Ibid.*, pp. 1–31.

18. Jack Rothman, personal communication, June 1972.

19. Social Planning Council of Metropolitan Toronto, "Comparative Study of Two Citizen Participation Models," Application for Research Grant, September 31, 1971.

20. For an analysis of the role of organizations in the dissemination and utilization of knowledge, see Ronald G. Havelock, ch. 6, pp. 1–40.

21. For a discussion of conferences devoted to research utilization, see Rensis Likert and Ronald Lippitt, "The Utilization of Social Science," in Leon Festinger and Daniel Katz, eds., *Research Methods in the Behavioral Sciences* (New York, Dryden Press, 1953), pp. 590–94.

22. Henry S. Maas, pp. 8–9.

23. Personal communication, May 1972.

24. Henry S. Maas, ed., *Five Fields of Social Service: Reviews of Research* (New York, National Association of Social Workers, 1966).

25. Alfred Kadushin, "Child Welfare," in Henry S. Maas, *Research in the Social Services*, pp. 13–69.

26. For example, Henry S. Maas, *Research in the Social Services*. Also, the National Association of Social Workers publishes *Abstracts for Social Workers* and *Social Work*, which occasionally include research review articles. Research review articles also appear in other professional journals such as *Welfare in Review*, *Social Service Review*, and *Child Welfare*.

27. Rensis Likert and Ronald Lippitt, in Leon Festinger and Daniel Katz, pp. 602–20; Alvin W. Gouldner, "Explorations in Applied Social Science," in Alvin W. Gouldner and S. M. Miller, eds., *Applied Sociology: Opportunities and Problems* (New York, Free Press, 1965), pp. 5–22.

28. For a detailed analysis of consultants as intermediaries between researchers and practitioners, see Ronald G. Havelock, ch. 1, pp. 1–40.

29. For a discussion of planning how to use evaluation consultants, see Tony Tripodi et al., *Social Program Evaluation*, ch. 5, "Use of Consultation," pp. 113–37.

30. Sidney E. Zimbalist, "The Research Component of the Masters Degree Curriculum in Social Work: A Survey Report," Ad Hoc Survey Committee on Research in the Graduate Curriculum of the Council on Social Work Education (Chicago, Jane Addams Graduate School of Social Work, September 1972).

Index